KATHLEEN ACKER RAMSEY

THE
GAME
OF LIFE

REDEFINING YOUR BELIEFS AND DISCOVERING YOUR TRUE POWER

THE GAME OF LIFE

REDEFINING YOUR BELIEFS
AND DISCOVERING YOUR TRUE POWER

KATHLEEN ACKER RAMSEY

To contact the author: www.thegameoflife101.com

ISBN: 979-8-9859652-7-8

DEDICATION

I would like to dedicate this book to all those that seek truth, desire freedom, and who are on a journey to create a world of love and compassion. May you have faith and courage to discover your true power by pulling up your anchor and breaking the chains of your mind. Set sail, my friend, and enjoy playing the Game of Life.

I wrote this book with purpose, to teach my boys how to steer their way through life's Game. Joe and Jack, you are my heart and soul, and you give me light to shine on the path I travel. This book is for you, to help you rise above when life seems to have lost its spark. You are my everything. I love you to the moon and back a trillion times.

To my parents: for your enduring love and guidance, teaching me to know right from wrong, to question all, and allowing me to discover my own path. You are a true blessing, thank you!

I give thanks and gratitude to God, my Creator, the Universe, my Source, for leading me through this Game of Life, giving me the courage to question everything I thought I knew, to walk by faith, not by sight, to know who I am, and for allowing me the opportunity to help others on their journey of self-discovery.

FOREWORD

Life truly is a Game. And while most people will shake their heads in confusion and displeasure over that concept, Kathleen Ramsey lifts the veil. What is seen beneath? A view reserved only for those determined enough to seek the truth.

Being in the spiritual and energetic arena for most of my career, I have learned the paramount principle that our thoughts, words, and deeds create the reality we all live within. While at times we may desire to exit the Game, or at least be temporarily sidelined when we experience sadness, fear, or despair, we must not risk getting caught in a low-vibration cascade of self loathing and wasted time. As we mingle with our peers (who often play this Game as poorly as we do), we collectively fail, fumble, and falter. Limiting affirmations become punishments, and our best efforts are reduced to a mediocre minimum. We must endeavor to first discover this truth about ourselves, and then, fix it.

Everything Kathleen wants you to know in this book, I have felt on an instinctual level for some time. Deep in my soul, at a primordial level, I recognized a flicker of hope that life was so much more than a cruel punishment. Once I was armed with that realization, I did everything I could to support this burgeoning, blossoming thought. I studied the great comparative evolutionists, further cementing this refined concept that all of humanity is in motion on one massive game board that each of us can learn to navigate with wisdom, efficiency, and fulfillment. Kathleen is also among the fringe dwellers, a deliverer of light and inspiration who will shake you out of slumber and reveal the intuition, progress, and peace you were always meant to have. Where the Game wants you to wallow in pain, this book teaches you to evolve and rise into harmony and balance. In short, this book gives you hope and purpose.

Upon meeting Kathleen, I saw a sweet, kind, hard-working ex-wife, mother, friend, contract creator, and daughter. At first, I thought she was just your everyday American woman doing what the Patriarch expected her to. Boy, was I wrong. I have never known someone as iron-willed and strong-minded as she is. Because of that strength, she is perfectly positioned to shatter the illusion of the matrix and guide us all through the work our highest beings have put us here to do.

Some of the topics here may trigger you, make you angry and perhaps even prompt you to slam this book closed as fast as you opened it. Don't succumb to that. Once you plateau on the discomfort of Kathleen's mind-blowing lessons, you will be forever changed. Pulling open the portal to the other side is risky and tenuous, but a different life is attainable, one that is full of joy, ease, contentment, homeostasis, and amazement.

This book is not just a one-time read; it is a lifelong study. Each time you allow the old paradigms, deeply buried limiting self-beliefs, subconscious faulty programming, and false narratives to bubble up to the surface and then *choose* to wash them away, you will understand the essence of this thesis. You will become proficient at the Game.

If you are truly ready to proclaim that everything you have been taught thus far is a lie and step into your own truth no matter what, now is the time to level up and invest in what Kathleen has laid out before you.

When you arrive at the end of this book, be prepared to re-examine all you've ever known. Allow yourself to embrace the unknown. Seek honesty and enlightenment. The more pliable we stay, the more flexible we can be while playing the Game. Our capacity to win widens when we can place our highest trust in the values of love, happiness, joy, ease, synchronicities, and windfalls of abundance. Stay open, stay fluid, and look upon this Game as if it's something you can't lose. The choice is yours. Play it wisely and with Kathleen's wisdom in hand.

Katie Boyd
www.kbmfc.com

CONTENTS

INTRODUCTION

Are you trying to figure out what life is all about? Are you searching for something that will move you closer to achieving your inner desires? Do you feel like you're just going through the motions to get by?

You have within you the ability to do extraordinary things and create a difference in your life and the lives of others. To achieve that ability, you must be willing to change your perspective. When you begin to view life as a Game, it generates a significant change in the way you perceive the world around you, your impact on it, and how you can transform the way you play.

This book is about inspiring people like yourself to raise their consciousness and knowledge about the Game of Life. We'll talk about having the courage to question your core *be.LIE. fs*, remove or stop old behaviors, release past traumas, and cultivate a willingness to let go.

We all get stuck in our comfort zones and go through the motions with no real direction from time to time. Exchanging a ho-hum life for an *extraordinary* life is all about self-realization and taking *intent.ional act.ions*. *Act.ions* that create a transformation into the person you were born to be.

This book is going to challenge you to be open to looking at life from an observer's view, to be okay with feeling uncomfortable at times, and to be willing to let go of things that we accept as status quo.

By learning to question and change your perspective, you will play the Game of Life with purpose and fulfillment by being mindfully aware of your existence. Life isn't about winning by beating someone else to the finish line (whether that line is about money, power, fame, glory, or status); it's about helping others in a positive way and leaving a loving imprint on your legacy.

Together we'll peel back the secrets on the rules of the Game, learn about the power of our thoughts, and demonstrate how setting *intent.ions* can transform our day-to-day existence. The *act.ions* you take each day, no matter how simple they might be, leave an impact on the lives of others and yourself. Do you want to leave a lasting positive impact to be *re.membered* by others? And to leave the world a better place than it was yesterday? If so, then this is the book to help you do that.

If you are ready to step into your true power and to become who you were born to be, then let's get started. First, we'll have a review of the rules and objective of the Game of Life, then we're going to start shifting your perceptions and building *intent.ional act.ions* that create a life of love, purpose, and service to others.

IN THE BEGINNING...

YOUR INTRODUCTION TO THE GAME

Buckle your seatbelt because this is going to be a bumpy ride. This book is going to question everything you know and challenge the way you look at everything around you and inside you. The world we live in isn't what we think or have been taught to think. There are more layers, more complexities, and far more truths to find as you dig a little—maybe a lot—deeper.

As the old saying goes, the truth shall set you free—but fair warning: it might blow your socks off first. Life is a Game, and it's a Game we have to play authentically and in concert with the Natural Laws if we want to achieve the ultimate prize: transforming to become our greatest selves and discovering our true power(s). Too often (and unknowingly) we let someone else play us or play *as* us, thus giving away our power and our desires, all because of an *ill.u.sion* created by others. We do this because we feel the need to fit in, follow old constructs, or just don't *inner-stand* (more on what that word means in a minute) how to take the wheel ourselves.

Stop doing that. Seriously, STOP NOW! There's a reason you were guided to pick up this book. The vibrational frequency inside you and around you set into motion your attr*act.ion* to the content in these pages. Trust your intuition and allow your inner core to be rattled and challenged because this is how you shift and see the world with new *eYes*. It's something we all must do in order to break the chains put upon us and play the Game of Life magnificently.

I know the concept of seeing life as a Game might be strange, but life is strange and ever-evolving. In movies like *Harry Potter* and *Men in Black,* there are two realms of reality, one that is hidden (in plain sight) to normal people and one that is open to people with powers (like awareness or knowledge). These are the kind of powers that help you see the Game of Life from an elevated view, as if you are in an airplane, and then make moves as your highest self.

It's pretty exciting to realize that by doing this, we could see the unseen things talked about in the movies and mentioned in the Bible. Would you want to be able to do that? What if you could use that other realm of reality to truly understand how the Universe works? What if you had the ability to control your life more than you ever thought possible? Would you want to know how? What if you had the opportunity to grow in consciousness and be part of a revolution that will change the course of our world? Would you choose to play or be played by someone else?

I know this all seems a bit far-fetched, but so did the idea of the entire world shutting down in a matter of weeks and coming to a standstill because of an unseen, creepy, and dangerous virus. Right now, while you are blithely living your life, there is a Game being played, whether you choose to be aware of it or not. You either learn to play consciously or get played by someone else; that choice is up to you. This book will be the guidebook to help you take back the reins of your life and create more meaning, depth, and purpose.

The journey might be overwhelming at times. It might be scary. But it's going to be one you will never regret taking because, in the end, you will be stepping into your best life with power, confidence, compassion, and love for self and all. This book teaches you to rise above the crushing weight of society's expectations and archaic ways of thinking. It's a liberating feeling when you begin to open your *eYe*s and see the world with a new perspective. It's like taking off a thick layer of clothes, then another layer, stripping down to your bare skin to see the true beauty within yourself. Together, we are pulling back the curtain on the Grand Wizard of Oz, the one who fabricated the *ill.u.sion* which forms a falsehood of fear in the Game we are all part of. Today, **right now**, it's time to peek behind the curtain and see the truth so that you can live life with authenticity.

This book will open your *eYe*s to what is going on all around you and within you. It will teach you how to set into motion *intent. ional act.ions* that shift your perception through your *e.motions*, thoughts, and *act.ions*. When you are *intent.ional*, every move you make has more meaning and more impact. When you are *intent.ional*, you put into motion a higher energy vibration frequency, which creates a ripple effect of positivity around you and inside you. Essentially, you create a new *tell.A.vision* channel for your life, one that has significance and depth. When you are *intent.ional*, you don't just change your life—you change everyone else's life, too. How? When you are *intent.ional*, your electromagnetic field becomes electrifying and highly charged and attracts the same vibe.

This book is more than just reading about how to play the Game. I will also give you helpful *act.ion* steps to create your inner greatness and true power. At the end of each chapter, you will find "Dash" *act.ions*, which are meant to fill the dash in your life, i.e., the time between the day you are born and the day you pass on. That dash is your one shot at living your best life. What you do and how you play that dash is what the Game is all about.

So, before you turn the next page and start this revolutionary life change, take a few deep breaths, focusing on the area of your heart (for more information on this technique, go to www. heartmath.org). Close your *eYe*s, go deep within, and know that everything is going to be okay. How do I know this for sure? Because this book is written with so much love for you and all the gifts you bring to this world! Every problem has a solution, and most of all, love and oneness are the reality of the Game!

Let's vibe this together!

THE RULES
OF THE GAME

THE OBJECT OF THE GAME

This adventurous Game has many twists and turns, ups and downs, and is an ongoing battle with your own inner conflict. Much like the games where you are tasked with saving a princess or crossing a finish line, this Game also requires engagement and learning the rules of the world in order to survive and triumph. Instead of a knight in shining armor rescuing a princess, however, in this Game, you are saving *yourself.*

Even though that's a serious undertaking, I want you to have fun with this, too. Whatever role you are playing right now, be it the Hero or the Victim or the Savior, you will discover more inner strength and courage by enjoying the Game.

COMPREHENDING THE GAME BOARD

Your Game board (essentially your life and self) may appear, on the surface, to be a chaotic mess right now. That's because you have unknowingly allowed someone else to control your personal court all this time. Maybe you thought someone would come save you or that you didn't have the ability to control your destiny. Every task you complete will help you clean up your board and thus, enjoy life as intended, with true power and love.

HOW TO WIN

Everyone makes it back home, but how they get there and what happens on their journey is 100% different from person to person. There are millions of ways to play and a thousand unique ways to make that journey. It's all about the vibe you bring to the Game.

WHAT'S INCLUDED

Society: Society plays by its own rules, rules that are designed to deceive us with *ill.u.sion*s, traps, tricks, and more. For instance, success, stardom, power, money—all seem like great goals to strive for, but those are just more examples of deception. What you have been taught is important may not be important at all. In order to level up, you have to see through that veil of deception and be aware of the traps that will delay you.

Successful players attract a vibe that elevates all the other players. The Game of Life isn't just about you. It's also about the collective consciousness that we work on jointly in order to raise the entire collective to a higher vibe, a higher consciousness, and thus, transform our world for the better.

Game Pieces: Each of us plays a part (game piece) in the Game. That piece has several different titles, whether that's mother/father, artist, doctor, trucker, president, teacher, manager, officer, athlete, movie star, friend, son/daughter, etc. Society tries to convince us that one title is higher than another when in reality we are all equal, regardless of our titles.

We can have several titles at the same time, depending on where we are in our journey. We have the power to change our game piece, meaning our title, whenever we desire. What if you started thinking of yourself as a leader instead of a follower? What if you gave yourself the title of business owner and made that leap from the 9-to-5 employee? As the good witch Glinda, in *The Wizard of Oz,* said, "You always had the power, my dear, you just had to learn it for yourself."

Re.member who you are, inside, because that remains, regardless of your gender, skin tone, nationality, religion, or title. We all have blood that flows through us, a heart that beats, lungs that breathe air. We are all spiritual beings with electromagnetic fields of energy and have a purpose to live as equals.

THE FOUR GOLDEN RULES OF THE GAME

There aren't a lot of rules in this Game, but there are four that I think are necessary, no matter what level you are on, who you are playing against/with, or where you are planning to go next.

1. **Do NO harm**—to yourself or others.

    a. **If you do harm to another** – give remedy.

        i. Harm is not hurt feelings. If a person's feelings are offended/hurt, they need to do inner healing. In other words, it's on them to clean up their own trauma/pain.

2. **Stay in honor at all times**—with yourself and others. Be respectful.

3. **All men and woman are equal**—all. There are no exceptions.

4. **Follow the Natural Laws**—a summary of some of the Natural Laws is provided in Chapter 1. Additional information on all the Natural and Universal Laws can be found in many other places; there are no limits to learning about these.

TRAPS AND OBSTACLES YOU MAY FACE

Don't expect the road to be a smooth journey from start to finish. Every journey has missed turns, detours, and breakdowns. These are opportunities for *growth,* which is what allows you to level up, so embrace these moments when you reach them.

1. **Repetition**: Whenever we experience a trauma or setback, we have a choice to either heal or repeat those lessons over and over until we finally heal and change.

2. **Perception**: If you look at an obstacle as hard, it's hard. If you look at it as a challenge to overcome, you will overcome it. Change the way you think about life and you change your life.

3. **Repeats**: Some lessons will repeat throughout your life at different levels in order to heal you at a deeper level. This goes beyond repetition. Maybe you were involved in an abusive relationship and kept choosing partners like that for years until you did the necessary inner work and healed that trauma. With repeats, you might meet another abusive person (maybe to a lesser degree) and are then tested to see if you learned your lesson and get out of this relationship at the beginning. This is where you learn to look for the red flags and read the other person's vibe so you can leave that relationship quickly. This allows you to attract a more loving and kinder person the next go-around.

4. **Triggers**: We tend to hold on to old pains/hurts, which keeps the past alive and causes it to boil to the surface when you are triggered in the present. You can then end up caught in a loop where the past becomes your present *and* your future.

5. **Spells**: We call it *spell.ing* for a reason—because *words* cast spells. If you say to yourself, *I am lucky*, you set a vibe to be lucky. If you tell yourself something is scary, your mind accepts that it's scary and makes you afraid to tackle it. This is beyond perception because this is in the words you speak mentally and aloud. If you change the word "scared" to "excited", then the moment you are fearing becomes an exciting opportunity for growth. Be mindful of low vibration words and switch to positive words, because then you set into motion the vibe that you seek.

Enjoy the Game!

Re.member: LOVE, GRATITUDE, HAPPINESS, KINDNESS, COMPASSION, & ACCEPTANCE!

CHANGE YOUR EMOTIONS

THE COMMENCEMENT OF THE GAME

Level 1 is all about learning how the Game works and seeing how you are currently playing it. It's about *inner.standing* your world and your role within it. Read this section with an open mind as you reexamine how the world works.

CHAPTER 1

COMPREHENDING THE GAME OF LIFE

"Don't speak *negatively* about yourself, *even as a joke*. Your body doesn't know the difference. Words are *energy and cast spells*, that's why it's called spelling. Change the way you *speak about yourself* and you can change your life. What you're not changing, you're also choosing."

BRUCE LEE

Have you ever played "peekaboo" with a baby? When you hide your face behind a blanket or a pillow, the baby thinks the face is gone because the baby doesn't realize that the face is just hidden temporarily, essentially masked. The disappearing act is an *ill.u.sion* in the baby's mind. That's what happens in the Game of Life for so many of us every single day. Our game piece, in other words, our self, is being shown something, maybe on *tell. LIE.vision* (look at the end of this chapter for a glossary of these unique words that are designed to make you think) that is being marketed to us as real life when, in reality, it's a grand *ill.u.sion* created by the controllers of society. Society wants us to think and see things, not as they truly are, but as the *ill.u.sion*s that have been created. It's only by seeing through that veil that you can be the one in charge of how you play the Game of Life and stop being fooled by the *ill.u.sion*s and deceptions going on around you.

Let's start with one of the most common (albeit innocent) lies the world continues to tell: Santa Claus. From birth, many of us are told that the jolly guy in the red suit is the one who brings the presents under the tree, who watches our behavior all year, and judges us accordingly. Adults know Santa Claus isn't real and that they are telling their children a lie. It's not a lie that's *intent.ionally* hurting anyone, but it is setting us up for *be.LIE. ving* things that aren't true.

I'm not here to bash Santa Claus, but to illustrate a point. I want you to go back in time for a moment and think about when you first learned Santa wasn't real. What was your *re.act.ion*?

- Did you think maybe Santa wasn't real but feared questioning authority (your parents) because you might not get any presents;

- or were you the kid who knew the truth before the other kids and wanted to spill the beans (thinking how did they not see the truth, yet it's so obvious to you);

- or were you the kid who *be.LIE.ved* with all your heart Santa had to be real because you saw him at the mall and on the *tell.LIE.vision*, therefore, he was indeed real?

How you answer the above actually tells you more about yourself than you may realize (more on that in a minute). Santa was the introduction to the lies we all have been told since the day we were born. At its core, the Santa story means that the world we live in is not at all what we think or thought.

Here's the problem with Santa Claus. When a lie like Santa is repeated, even if the *intent.ions* are good, it becomes a core part of our *be.LIE.f* system (what we *be.LIE.ve* is a truth that is actually based upon a **lie**). The lie then becomes embedded in our mind and is accepted as a truth. As you read this book, I challenge you to choose to have an open mind and be receptive to new ways of looking at the world around you.

We were all lied to, not just about Santa, but about a lot more (and I'm not just talking about the Easter Bunny and the Tooth Fairy). *Re.member*, the world is essentially a stage, and the things you are seeing and hearing are whatever the "director" at the moment wants you to see and hear.

So how do you know if something is real or true? Start by trusting your heart. Your heart has a brain and is a connection to your intuition. Your heart sees through the *ill.u.sion*.

I have been down many rabbit holes searching for truth, and my advice to you is this: Whatever really resonates with you as true is your path. If it is uncomfortable information (maybe a criticism you don't want to hear), but your heart knows something about it is true, then TRUST your heart. On the other side of that, if something is a *no* in your heart and your gut is saying *this isn't true*, trust your heart. Don't blindly *be.LIE.ve* something or someone outside of you. After all, the only purpose of *tell.LIE.vision* is and has always been to tell us someone else's vision of the world they want us to see and *be.LIE.ve*. Case in point: just because you saw Santa on *tell.LIE.vision* doesn't make him real.

We're talking about Santa and the way society works because I want you to see the big picture before you get into specifics about the Game of Life. This book is all about helping you understand how life works and how you can "play" better by becoming your best self. When you play the Game mindfully, your life is richer, you are happier and more grounded. Play it mindlessly and you are doomed to make the same mistakes over and over again. By thinking of life as a Game, you can develop a strategy, become more thoughtful (i.e., *intent.ional*) in your moves, and most of all, have fun doing it.

So, before you pick your game piece, I want you to grasp how the Game works and the rules that are working behind the scenes. We have been playing this Game not knowing the rules for way too long and making a lot of mistakes. Time to stop that and start creating.

Let's start with some of the Natural Laws because these are the guideposts for how everything truly works in life. *Inner-standing* these will help you comprehend how to create the world you desire.

First, a note: There are dozens of books and videos on the Natural Laws. That's because inner-standing Natural Laws is key to playing the Game successfully. These are the laws I find most critical in playing the Game.

1

THE LAW OF
ONENESS

We are connected by our heartbeats. The heartbeat starts life and ends life. While we are alive, our hearts all beat and connect to each other as part of the vibrational rhythm of life. Whenever you see another person, you are essentially seeing yourself, just in a different body. Ponder on that for a moment. I know you're thinking that's nuts, that there's no way that mean guy at the grocery store or that screaming woman is you—but we are all from the same source.

The essence of Oneness is that we appear to be separate beings. Just as a tree is made up of roots, trunk, branches, leaves, and fruit—all those pieces individually appear different, yet they are also part of the whole and work together as one. As leaves fall to the ground, they go back to the soil and feed the roots and help the entire tree system. We do the same with what we release into the world. We have more commonality between us than just breathing the same air—we are, in our roots (our source), the same person in a different version. Our hearts, therefore, beat as one.

THE LIE THE WORLD TELLS YOU

It's you against "them," whoever the "them" is in the Game. Whether it's the poor versus the rich or this race versus that race, the elderly versus the young…the list is endless. They're "different" from you and thus lesser than or separate from you. That's hogwash. Divorce that thinking right now. We're all connected, and when you inner-stand the **Law of Oneness**, your perception shifts.

THE TRUTH YOU SHOULD KNOW

You should never look at others as bad or evil; society has taught us to judge ourselves and others. Accept others and know that their purpose on earth is to have an experience. Perhaps they have a karmic debt to pay and are being given the opportunity to be the victim this lifetime, or maybe even the perpetrator. Perhaps your kindness will aid them in choosing differently. We all lead by example, so *shine your light.*

YOUR DASH ACT.ION

Choose to see others as a mirror of you, but in a different body. Then pause. Take a moment and pretend to be them; imagine you are playing their role. How does it feel? How would you want you to treat you? Realize that your words, act.ions, and thoughts affect the collective whole of you. They are a boomerang, reflecting back on you.

LIVING IN THE DASH

Every one of us will have a dash "-" on our tombstones between the day we were born and the day we die. The Dash Act.ions in this book are designed to help you play the Game of Life and live your greatest moments in that dash! Enjoy!

2

THE LAW OF VIBRATION (ATTRACTION)

Vibe it up because vibrational frequency is in everything! Words, sounds, light, numbers, sacred geometry, symbols—they all carry a vibrational frequency. Science shows we have an electromagnetic energy field that can be measured three feet from our heart. This field is affected by thoughts, *e.motions*, food, who we surround ourselves with, and many other factors. We attract or match up to the vibration we put out.

Have you ever felt really good around a place or person? That's because you are picking up on their vibe. Simplified, the energies and *act.ions* we send out into the world vibrate throughout that same world, both in good ways and bad. The words and feelings you send out are essentially vibrations in motion. That means if you send out vibes of abundance, you will create and receive abundance in return. When combined with the first Law of Oneness, you realize that your vibrations impact others, and come right back to you, with the same impact, good or bad. These laws work just as the cells in the body do. A single cell can affect all the other cells around it, either causing *dis.ease* to spread or curing you.

THE LIE THE WORLD TELLS YOU

That we don't have that much of an impact on others or on the world at large.

THE TRUTH YOU SHOULD KNOW

In truth, we're all one giant ripple effect, no matter how small or large of a stone we think we are. Think about the vibrational frequency you are putting out—if it's negative, imagine that negativity rippling across a pond of people, contaminating each of them like a swath of red tide. Then think about having a positive vibrational frequency, and imagine the joy that will spread across that same pond. You choose your vibe in every moment, so choose wisely.

YOUR DASH ACT.ION

Before you leave the house for the day, set the vibe you want to have in your heart and mind, visualize your day, and see the impact you can have on the others in your bubble. When you set your *intent.ions* for the day, include the thought, "It's a great day!" because that directs your *e.motions* and how you will respond versus *re.act*. Visualize the day with amazing outcomes and lots of love. Then sit back and notice how your day goes.

The Universe responds to the vibrational frequency you put out. It does not distinguish between your personal desires or wants, or figure them into the equation. The Universe only knows the vibe you are generating at the moment. Example: If you desire a new job with better pay, yet your vibration is one of lack or feeling unworthy, that is what it will attract more of. Feel the vibe you want. Actually, **feel** it. Even if you can only do this, for a few minutes each day at first, every time you do this it begins to shift your vibe because your thoughts create the *e.motion* of that vibe, which then creates the inspired *act.ions* you need to take.

3

THE LAW OF
INSPIRED ACT.ION

This is the get-off-your-ass-and-do-something law. Seriously—inspired *act.ion* is all about *intent. ional*ly putting your inner desires into *act.ion*. It's awesome to dream about buying that big house or finding the perfect soulmate or achieving your dream career, but it's not going to be handed to you. There are many books and speakers who say, "Visualize and it's yours." But they leave out the reality part of this critical Natural Law: **You have to take inspired *act.ions* in the direction of your desired outcome.**

THE LIE THE WORLD TELLS YOU

The world says good things come to those who wait. Waiting doesn't get you anywhere except stuck in the same place. Re.member Sleeping Beauty? She just lies there, sleeping, waiting on her prince to come.

THE TRUTH YOU SHOULD KNOW

News flash—that's not how it works. No prince or princess is going to come along and rescue you. Choose to perceive this as the fun part of being actively involved in this Game of Life. The kiss from the prince isn't another person changing your life—it's your inner awakening that lights the fire inside you.

YOUR DASH ACT.ION

When you have a feeling inside or a gentle nudge to do something, don't procrastinate. **Do it now**. That nudge is your inner self, guiding you to have trust and faith to take that first leap.

4
THE LAW OF RHYTHM

This Law is about the natural rhythm in life, in us, in nature. Nature has patterns of life that are repeated, and so do you. Think of a moment when everything flowed so well and was smooth and easy. Now think of a time when nothing went right. The common theme there is the rhythm that was inside you at the time. It's the flow that stems from your thoughts, directing your *e.motions*, which lead to *act.ions*. You can change these patterns and imprint new, positive patterns that change your life to flow with ease. Get into the flow.

THE LIE THE WORLD TELLS US

We are not really taught the importance of going with the flow. Society wants to keep you in a pattern of constant chaos instead of encouraging you to create a flow of coherence. It's like trying to swim against the current. You end up exhausted and no further along than when you started. We have been programmed to have a rhythm that runs to someone else's beat rather than moving with the beat of our heart and of Earth.

THE TRUTH YOU SHOULD KNOW

When you work and live within the natural rhythm, life just flows easier. Trust your intuition to guide you throughout your day.

YOUR DASH ACT.ION

Start your day by setting your *intent.ions* to get into a good rhythm (something we talk about in more depth in Chapter 10). Do this by making a list of things that will help you get this rhythm into motion.

Wake up at the same time every day (this creates a rhythm to your days). Visualize the Game piece you desire to be, then see/feel/taste it. Choose the *act.ions* that will help fulfill your *intent.ions*. For example, if you visualize yourself as a fit person, choose a workout. If you visualize yourself as successful at your job, take an *act.ion* that moves you closer to being that, like taking a class or reading up on strategies others use in that line of work.

Bonus Dash Act.ion: Use it or lose it. If you have crap sitting in your home you are not using, give it to someone who can use it. Otherwise, you stop the flow of energy for receiving. It is not only kind and loving to give, it benefits you in return.

5

THE LAW OF PERPETUAL TRANSMUTATION OF ENERGY

Everything in us and our world is energy in motion; everything is in constant movement. Energy cannot be created nor destroyed; it transforms from one state to another. Your thoughts create *e.motions* (this is energy in motion). With this energy, you direct your life because you are manifesting it with your thoughts (keep those thoughts positive and it will create more positivity!). Be careful what you think about and how you *re.act* to things that happen throughout your day. Thoughts (formless energy) are constantly flowing into the material world (by *e.motions*) and taking form (through *act.ions*).

THE LIE THE WORLD TELLS US

Society wants us to be.LIE.ve we have limits to our abilities, power, dreams, and desires. We are taught to feel helpless, to stand down to authority, to play small. Who are you to think big?

THE TRUTH YOU SHOULD KNOW

The truth is simple: Who are you *not* to think BIG? You have within you the ability and power to be extraordinary, limitless, and powerful in a positive wave of energy. Energy is a state of mind, so be mindful. When you raise your vibration, it transforms lower vibrations. When you walk into a room that is low vibes and you bring forth happy, loving vibrations, it will be felt and help lift others up to a higher vibe. This is a key in the Game of Life.

YOUR DASH ACT.ION

When someone triggers you, you undoubtedly want to attack back with yelling or proving you're right. Instead, **harness** that energy and **transform** it into a loving response. Maybe the person had a bad day, or they have an anxious/angry/negative vibe due to something that happened to them previously and your words triggered a *re.act.ion* in them. Showing compassion and kindness toward them helps you shift your vibe and might help shift theirs, too. That is a win. Either way, don't allow their energy to transmute through you. ***You control your responses and re.act.ions***. If you allow them to hurt you, why are you doing that? Don't carry that negative energy around with you.

6

THE LAW OF POLARITY

This Law is based on opposites. We have ups, we have downs; we have happiness, we have sadness. There is evil and good, love and fear. As far right as you can go, the same distance goes to the left, meeting back where you started. The never-ending eternity of life is found in the middle where we, for that moment, see good meet evil and love meet fear on the dance floor. It is the uniting of the opposites that brings balance. Polarity, thus, is essential to having true power within.

We need these opposites in order to help us learn, grow, evolve, and transform. How do you know success without failure? Love without loss? Pain without hurt? Happiness without sadness.

The Game of Life, like all games, has moments of joy and heartache. We learn through experience, and in the process of going through these opposites, we arrive in the middle, at a place of neutrality. Only then can we rise above to create ascension and discover a new level of *inner.standing* of all of the Natural Laws.

The Game of Life is all about finding the peace and balance of the Natural Laws, and then creating a flow for energy.

THE LIE THE WORLD TELLS US

Opposites are a bad thing; we hear that all day on the news. We are taught to hate the opposite of whatever they conjure up that week: another country, group, religion, etc. Don't fall into this trap.

THE TRUTH YOU SHOULD KNOW

Opposites help us learn, appreciate, and grow. For example, *live* is *evil* spelled backwards, which makes them mirror opposites. If we don't understand evil, how do we know goodness? The Law of Polarity helps us evolve and inner-stand life so we can rise to new heights and complete the cycle.

YOUR DASH ACT.ION

Learn to question why you think an opposite is bad. Society sets traps to sway our opinions to *be.LIE. ve* that a group or type of person or whatever is bad or good. *Re.member*, you own the script, you create your life, and it's up to you to seek knowledge and wisdom to look at the situation differently, and with righteousness from your heart and soul.

7

THE LAW OF GENDER

We have feminine and masculine energy, regardless of our identity. The masculine energy impregnates and plants our feminine energy with the seed of an idea, which gives birth to our *e.motions*/feelings and leads to our *act.ions*. The time it takes for the seed to give birth to the idea is governed by this law. Some gestation periods of ideas are fast, others take time to penetrate our soul's desire. Everything that is created began as a seed of thought, nurtured with balance of both energies.

The other side of this Law is that when the logical, practical side of our brain (masculine) is out of balance it shows up as control, anger, and conflict. When our spiritual, intuitive, nurturing side (feminine) is out of balance it shows up as vulnerability and weakness. Learning to align your logical side with your spiritual side is a major lesson in the Game. If your Game is played with too much of one or the other, chaos takes over. Play the Game mindfully aware of which one is dominant in you and set your intention to bring balance by adding a bit of the other gender to the flow. By doing that, you are planting the seed of your idea.

THE LIE THE WORLD TELLS US

Society teaches us to get frustrated when things don't happen in the time frame we think they should. Let go of that control and let it flow.

THE TRUTH YOU SHOULD KNOW

Trust with emotion/feeling and know that your idea will manifest, instead of stressing about the "when". In doing so, you create a nurturing vibration, and your desire will manifest faster. If it doesn't happen in the time frame you anticipated, trust that the Universe is working for your best interests and it will happen in perfect time. Don't doubt it.

YOUR DASH ACT.ION

Make a list of the ideas you have and what resonates with you for your future. Visualize it, think about the *act.ion* steps needed to make it a reality, and review it each day and let it grow. By repeating this, you are training your brain to manifest this outcome for you, in time.

With the basics of the Natural Laws in mind, we can start delving deeper into how they work and how to live them with intention. I intend for this book to be easy to comprehend, and the practices I talk about to be easily implemented. If you're ready to transform every area of your life, turn the page, and let's get started!

CHANGE THE WAY YOU SEE THESE WORDS

Words are a puzzle that you can deconstruct and better understand on your path to creating a positive vibe in your life,

Act.ion: Act = do something + ion = an electric charge creates the result of. The *act.ions* you take are the result of the choices you make.

Be.LIE.f: The word belief has the word LIE built into it. We have to reprogram ourselves and choose to shift from within and question all our *be.LIE.fs*.

Cult.ure: Cult = a particular form or system of worship; unorthodox or voodoo; devotion to person, idea, object, movement; Ure = effect, operation, procedure, practice; *Cult.ure* = practice of worship of an idea, object, person, or movement.

Dis.ease: When the body is not in a state of normalization, it creates *dis.ease*, which can lead to health issues, or unease mentally when your body is not in alignment with your soul.

E.motion: This is energy in motion.

Empowerment: E (energy). Power (ability/authority to influence or change an outcome). Ment (control) = you have the ability/authority to change and control your energy.

eYe: Also called the Third *eYe*. To visualize or imagine something without actually seeing it with your *eYe*s; the mental faculty of conceiving imaginary or recollecting scenes; intuition. Between your *eYe*s lies the pineal gland where the center of both *eYe*s meet to form imagination.

Ill.u.sion: Ill = do evil to; hurtful; morally evil; wicked. U = thou or you. Sion = imaginary place or state of; act of; result of. To hurt or do evil to you as a result of an act. Illusions are the constructs of society that are designed to keep you from seeing the healthy truth.

Inner-standing: This means connecting within (inner) yourself at a cellular level so that you can get to the heart (truth) of the matter; trusting (standing) in your intuition.

Intent.ions: Intent = a purpose, aim, goal or desire + ions = an electric charge creates the result. Your desire or purpose creates the result.

Re.act: Re (to do again). Act (to take or do something) = to act again based on past experience.

Re.member: Re (to do again). Member (the entire body, mind, soul is one) = all the members of the body are one body.

Shift: This is the brain's way to adapt or to change behavior, thoughts, and feelings/emotion to a new way of thinking, feeling, behaving, and acting. It's the ability to see what you're doing doesn't work and change to a new concept, approach, and adapt to situations differently than before.

Tell.A.vision: Society's way of showing the world an *ill.u.sion* or vision of the way things *appear* to be; someone else's vision of how they want the Game to play out. Also known as *tell.LIE. vision* = which means telling a lie, not the truth, in order to create deception.

Under.stand: This means to stand under another or to consent to be judged by someone.

Vibe(s): The vibration frequency wave you're emitting, it's your electromagnetic field of energy.

CHAPTER 2

LOOK AT THE BOARD STRATEGICALLY

"The secret of change is to focus all of your energy, not on fighting the old, but building the new."

SOCRATES

One of the hardest lessons in life is learning to let go of other people that we love. We let go in many ways and for many reasons, be it because of a death, a move, a breakup, a new job, an argument, or simply growing apart. Sometimes it takes years to let go; sometimes there is so much pain that comes from the end of a relationship that you need to speak to a professional to help you process it. That's totally okay. It is said that when we cry it's our soul's way of cleansing itself of pain. Give yourself grace if you want to cry. Let it out, embrace it, and let it flow down the drain.

I had a crash course in letting go over a three-year time frame when my dad, brother, Nana, aunt, and a kind dear friend all passed away. In that same time frame, I moved five times, saying goodbye to friends I would never see again and leaving jobs I loved. Many times, I felt all alone in a strange new world. All of this occurred while I was going back to graduate school and getting married to a man who would end up physically abusing me. Eventually I developed a strategy for my life, left the abusive man, and let go of the material world I had become accustomed to.

I learned so much about myself during that time period and went through a full range of *e.motions* as I learned to let go and embrace change, including anger, which remained a part of me for way too long. When we let go of someone else, we always lose a part of ourselves and have to rebuild those pieces (fragments) of ourselves. Sometimes a loss leaves holes in our heart and scar tissue forms over that space, making us forever changed. I don't think anyone ever "masters" this lesson of letting go. The only thing you can do is learn to have grace for yourself, to honor the pain you are feeling by fully facing it, and to take a moment to embrace the lessons you have learned and the new strength you have gained.

Embrace yourself, face whatever you fear, be open to healing and change. I promise, it's not as scary as you imagine, and a wonderful life awaits you.

Inner-standing and abiding by the Universal Laws we just discussed in Chapter 1 gives you an opportunity to increase your vibe, and in the process, evolve your consciousness, which helps you cope with losses more gracefully. As you do that, you *re.member* things at a cellular level. At that point, you have the choice to do one of two things: heal past traumas, pains, and *e.motions*, or hold on to them and keep banging your head on the wall asking, *Why does this keep happening to me?*

Be mindful of the words you use when you are going through a painful period. Choosing to heal and move forward is a key step to moving through the Game of Life positively. You don't forget those pains and traumas; you simply learn to move forward without them.

See the Impact of the World Around You

The traumas and the issues you are facing are basically your opportunities to level up. Look around you and be mindful of the visual clues you are receiving. Clues are signs from the Universe designed to grab your attention and teach you something. Ask yourself, *How do these thoughts make me* feel? *How are these thoughts impacting me, physically, mentally, and spiritually? Are they true?*

For the purposes of this book, I will use the word God, but please feel free to insert Creator, Buddha, Source, or whatever Higher Power you accept as true.

For example, when I watched the movie *The Passion of the Christ*, I felt heartache when I saw the merciless punishment Jesus endured. I stopped the movie, dropped to my knees, cried, and said, "Dear God, how can someone do this to another human being? How can this kind of behavior be in me?"

The scene of the beating of Jesus exploded and intensified my realization that I have beaten others down with my words. Not *intent.ionally*, because I never mean to hurt anyone. Yet it happens. If you were on the receiving end of my words or *act.ions* and I hurt you, please forgive me. I am very sorry, I do love you, thank you.

Watching the pain Jesus suffered at the hands of others reminded me to be more mindful and *intent.ional* with my words and cognizant of how I impact other people. Whether we admit it or not, we have all said hurtful words or done hurtful *act.ions* to another person. It may not be with switches or swords, but we hurt others, especially loved ones. In our mind, we sometimes rationalize that the other person deserved it and then we feel justified in our behavior, or we think the hurt we inflicted was minor. That is not for us to decide or judge. When you are hurting someone emotionally or physically, you are hurting someone, period. There is no bigger or deeper or more traumatic hurt. Hurt is hurt; it's all equal. *Re.member* the Rule we mentioned earlier to always "Stay in Honor."

A technique I practice to cleanse, heal, and remove negative, toxic vibes and treat people/things with more love and respect is *Ho'oponopono.* This is a powerful spiritual healing technique from Hawaii that teaches you to free yourself from low vibration problems, feelings, and experiences of trauma and pain that are not serving your highest most divine self/purpose, which is love. It brings a vibe to your life of love and compassion with words. The words you speak are simple yet powerful and effective: *"I'm sorry, please forgive me, thank you, I love you."*

Ho'oponopono is a Game changer, I promise. Make it a mantra, a chant, and apply it on a regular basis. You can use Ho'oponopono for anything in your life because we are all connected and everything is interconnected. This includes Mother Earth, bugs, tables, people, chairs...everything. If you hurt something, use Ho'oponopono. Doing so will help you treat all things with respect.

A NOTE ABOUT ABUSE

An abusive *act.ion* is a person causing fear and harm to another person. Abusers are titled villains, but a person is not born as a villain; we are all born innocent as babies, then fear, hurt, or trauma happen and creates a shift inside them, we will refer to as a trigger. For some that trigger may cause an abusive *act.ion* to occur. Something happened in the person's life that caused them to *re.act* in this manner. Knowing that doesn't mean you stay—it means you recognize this behavior and move forward by removing yourself in a loving, safe way.

I have been in an abusive situation before. I made a plan to remove myself safely, and in the process walked away from money and material things, and everything turned out for the better. When I was ready, I helped other women do the same by volunteering at abuse crisis organizations.

I learned, and will remind you, that you aren't here to fix that person; that's the other person's job (*re.member*, "it's not them, it's you" works both ways).

You attracted that relationship to your life in order to learn from it and gain perspective. However, you have a duty to love and honor yourself and safely remove yourself from any situation that causes you harm. Our Creator gave us the right to be free and to have free choice. The rule to do no harm to another includes no harm to ourselves. Honor thyself always, this is a major lesson in life.

Check Your Vibe

Happiness is a state of mind that creates a high vibration and gives you a different perspective on the Game of Life. Think of the sky. The sky is always there and so is happiness. Sometimes clouds cover the sky and we can't see it (or our own happiness). However, we always have the power to part those clouds. Like Moses parted the sea, you can part the clouds in your life and *choose* to be happy. It is a choice, a state of mind.

The happier you are, the higher your vibe, or in other words, it increases your frequency vibration of your electromagnetic field to **attract** that same frequency to you, like a magnet attracts metal. A happy state of mind will attract people and events that in turn draw happiness to you. When you tap into a high vibe, you create a flow that also inspires everyone around you to feel happy. Do you know someone that makes you happy to be near them? Think of it like a spark of electricity that lights up a room of people to create a joyful and happy experience.

As I mentioned earlier, the words you speak carry a vibration frequency. The old saying "be careful what you think" came about because thoughts have a vibration that is felt by those around you. Add in the *e.motions* you are feeling and you are creating energy in motion (*e.motion*).

E.Motion is energy in motion.

We are taught by society to feel envy, be judgmental, or feel dissatisfaction with our place in life and to gossip and bash other people who achieve greater things than us. Do you know someone who is petty, jealous, or always blaming others for their *act.ions* or feelings? We all do it at one time or another—but that also means we can all *stop* feeling those *e.motions* and shift into positive thoughts and *e.motions*.

We are programmed to compete against each other, but the Game of Life isn't about competing, it's about cheering each other on. When you look at someone who has achieved and received much success, do you get jealous? Or do you think, *I am happy for that person*? Set your intention to be happy for the other person, and then use that energy to impact your own life in a positive way. When you view the other players in the Game from a positive perspective, your attitude about succeeding in the Game increases your ability to succeed as much, if not more, than the other players.

When we remove competition from the thought process and shift to celebrating others' success, it attracts success to us.

However, if you feel jealous, threatened, or angry toward the other players, you are actually feeding your subconscious mind the message that *you* are not worthy and that you are lacking something, therefore, you cannot achieve that same success that they have received. That affects the vibe inside you and how you see the world around you. The opposite holds true in an even bigger way. If you are super excited for the other player(s), you are telling yourself, *That is possible for me too!!!*

Evolving your consciousness and increasing your vibe starts with creating a mental shift. Say to yourself:

"Let me see that differently."

Literally just stop, take a breath, and say those words to yourself. *Let me see that differently.*

Doing this teaches you awareness of your own thoughts and the impact your thoughts/*e.motions*/feelings/*act.ions*/words have on you, those around you, and the entire collective oneness of the Universe. You will notice a change or shift inside and realize you have the power to create who you desire to be and whether you respond in anger or with love.

Re.member, empowerment = E (energy). Power. Ment (control), meaning you create the power to control your energy. That's what this book is about—teaching you how to make those mental shifts that create more positive, *intent.ional* thoughts, and learning to respond rather than *re.act*. If you think you're too old to learn how to do something new, let me tell you that you definitely aren't.

When you first learn to drive a car, it takes a while to figure out when to shift gears or when to slow down/speed up. After you do it a hundred times, the process becomes second nature. Our mental shifts happen the same way.

Society teaches us that people don't change, and to shame those that step outside the box of "normal." When we change and do things different then the "approved" ways of society, we are called names, told to just be like the other players.

Elon Musk said in an interview, "Given the chance, people would rather die than change." Ponder on that. If we are not changing, we are dying. So, embrace change because life is about change in every moment. No day is the same, and you should be thankful for that opportunity!

If you never see things differently, you end up repeating the same patterns over and over again. Just as if you are playing a video game and keep repeating the same level over and over again (instead of leveling up), you don't learn how to overcome the monsters. Aren't you tired of repeating the same level?

I get it that you might be afraid of change or of looking at the world through a different lens or even seeing things from a new perspective. Society has pulled us into a hypnotic rhythm of doing as we're told, not standing out, and to be like everyone else. Put on your big girl or boy panties because once you have the courage to face your fears and are willing to be different, you realize it was silly to be so scared about that thing you feared, whether it's getting on a plane for the first time or apologizing to someone you hurt or standing up to authority. Whatever that fear is, face it head on. In the process, you become stronger, wiser, more empathetic, and compassionate. You then create a better, stronger, and more *intent.ional* vibe, which becomes your highest, best self.

To me, one of the most spiritual movies ever written is *The Wizard of Oz*. In that movie, everyone is afraid of the Wicked Witch and the flying monkeys until Dorothy comes along and lands her house on one witch, killing her and freeing the Munchkins. Then she throws water (the water of life) on the Wicked Witch, which sets the monkeys free. The Munchkins and monkeys rejoice in happiness (they have let go of their fear and the chains/control on their minds). Then Dorothy goes to Oz. Everyone there is afraid of the Wizard until Toto pulls back the curtain and shows them that the great wizard is just a little old man. He's nothing to fear at all and is only an *ill.u.sion*, a deception of the mind.

Embrace yourself, face whatever you fear, be open to healing and change. I promise, it's not as scary as you imagine, and a wonderful life awaits you.

Each of the characters had a lesson to learn, something that would heal their pasts and give them a brighter future. They had to realize that what they were seeking didn't come from another person or wizard, but rather was *already inside each of them.* Going to Oz gave them the opportunity to see it differently. The lion was already courageous, the scarecrow was already smart, and the tin man was already loved. For Dorothy, her lessons were about finding a feeling of belonging and home. By the end of the movie, she realizes home is already inside us all, Dorothy included.

Go within, find your shining attributes, and discover that courage, abundance, and wisdom are already flowing through you with grace and all you have to do is embrace and release those attributes into the world. The more you make that shift to see what is already within you, the more you will find love for yourself and others.

As we are tested, we level up more, which means facing new fears and challenges. However, doing the things I talk about in this book gives you the skills to deal with whatever happens, with more confidence and grace. Taking a moment to say, "*Let me see that differently,*" can change everything. Recently, I was having a disagreement with my mom and I realized the conversation was triggering me. I took a deep breath and said, "Mom, I'm sorry, but I need a minute. I'll call you back." It wasn't anything that my mother was doing—it was yesterday's pains inside me that were being triggered. She didn't need to change what she was saying; I needed to change how I *perceived* her words. This *act.ion* of taking time to look within is key because it gives you the opportunity to heal a prior event and move forward. Questioning our triggers and taking a moment to process them opens us to heal and undo the past.

Take a look at this symbol. Do you see it differently if you turn the book upside down? Sideways? If you look at it close up or from far away? Our perception can change if we try a new and different angle.

It's Not Them—It's Me

When you can take a step back and see the Game board from another vantage point, you can have so many powerful, life-changing realizations. The biggest realization is simple: ***I'm not a victim. I have power and control over my re.act.ions.***

When you approach life with a positive, *intent.ional*, healing vibe, it gives you even more control, and that has a tenfold effect on the people around you.

We talked about rhythm in the last chapter, and how things can have a natural, easy flow if you stop trying to control them so much and open yourself to more positivity. Using Ho'oponopono and reciting, *"I'm sorry, please forgive me, thank you, I love you,"* can create a rhythm of love and forgiveness because you start healing you instead of blaming the other person. That in turn attracts more love and abundance. Do it now and notice what happens!

THE TRUTH YOU SHOULD KNOW

It has never been about someone outside of you; it is one hundred percent about you. You have the power and control to shift how you choose to see everything and everyone. Choosing to see things from a different vantage point allows you to have control.

Plus, when you choose to see things differently, you change the Game you're playing, it feels empowering inside, and you encourage others to see the Game differently too.

YOUR DASH ACT.ION

Take a pause, look at the situation/game board. Don't underestimate the importance of pausing. We are in a go-go-go world, and sometimes we forget to take a breath before we respond. Learn to pause. I promise, it will be a useful strategic move for you.

If you are in the middle of a disagreement, try this little trick that helps you shift from being emotional (*re.act.ion*) to being logical (response): think of a math problem like 4 x 44 = ____. Doing this creates a right brain/left brain shift. You can't stay mad (emotional) when logic is presented (math). Try it.

Bonus Dash Act.ion: Whenever a situation comes up that you think is bad/sad/dark/poor, try to (either in the moment or later) start reflecting on what you think you saw. Question it with loving *eYe*s. Even if you or society views it as a horrible situation, ask yourself: *Is this a lie or is it true?* Question what you hear and see because just like Santa, many things are NOT what they appear to be on the surface.

AN IMPORTANT CONCEPT TO PONDER

In the Game of Life, stop trying to prove your worth to others and stand firm in knowing, feeling, and trusting you are worthy of all you desire and more. Thinking small about yourself is a trap that will keep you stuck in a lower vibe. You are worthy. The other person is not tuned into your channel. When you try to prove yourself to someone else, you lower your vibe and change from your vibe to theirs.

Seek those who vibe with you, not against you—that's what *being in the flow* means. Send love to those who hold you back, and let go of them. Maybe losing you from their life might cause them to grow internally and be part of their evolution as a human. Don't hold on to someone too long for the wrong reasons, because you are stopping both them and you from growing. Letting go is a release that allows you *both* to evolve.

CHAPTER 3

BUILDING AN UNBEATABLE STRATEGY

"Our path is like a giant circle with no beginning and no end. We are eternal—our Spirits can never die or be destroyed. We are fellow travelers in the game of life and our destinies are intertwined. Don't be afraid of shining a light. Don't be afraid of being powerful. Don't be afraid of being more special."

—DELORES CANNON

I start and end each day by reading my Game Plan, (along with the Our Father prayer). In my statement, I ask my past or future self to send me a message that I will recognize (and make it obvious so I don't miss it).

I command myself to be receptive to those messages even when there's a lot going on in my life and I've seen it work more than once. One time a friend of mine who lived in another country was going to be in the States for a month. She had asked me to come meet her and her family. At first, I didn't see that happening because I had too much going on. As the time drew closer to her departure date, I had a strong feeling urging me to go see her, so I reached out and asked when she was leaving. By coincidence, she had extended her stay by a week. We talked on a Tuesday, but I had a feeling that I needed to be there by Friday so I booked a flight for Thursday.

Before I left, she told me to pack a swimsuit because they were renting a boat while I was there. She explained that coincidently (I trust all coincidences are fate) a few of her friends were going to be in town as well and wanted to get a boat for the day. Even though I had never met her friends, I had a feeling this was synchronicity and all supposed to happen.

When I arrived on Thursday, I had dinner with her and her family. We talked non-stop for hours. The next day was beyond perfect. Even though I had never met these people before, there was an instant familiarity and a positively powerful vibe between us, as if we had all met on this day long ago on a soul level. We were finishing each other's sentences, and it felt more like a reunion than a first meeting. I have only had that happen with a few people in my life. As the day came to an end, there was a feeling that we each had a mission and we would meet again someday. Throughout the day, I experienced several moments of serendipity and realized my past/future-self had sent my now-self the gift of this day.

A month later, I knocked a journal to the floor and when I picked it up, I found an entry from a year earlier. On the page, I had written about a dream I had where I was on a boat with friends and having such a great day that I didn't want it to end because it seemed like we had a mission of some kind. Coincidence? I don't think so. A few days later, I noticed I had posted a picture months earlier on my vision board of an actual moment that took place that day. That was a profound experience for me. Was it another coincidence? I am positive that my future-self planted a seed in my past that took a year to grow and be birthed/bloom. That's the Law of Gender at work.

Plan Your Vibe Before You Start

Do you realize that your vibe introduces you before you even speak? Think about that for a second. What vibe do you think you are giving off when you walk into a room? Happiness or sadness? Compassion or blaming? Trust or doubt?

When you give off a vibe, others tap into it, and vice versa. Tapping into the vibe around us happens all day long, through emails, calls, meetings, in person. We literally pick up on the electromagnetic fields of others. I'm sure you've sensed a vibe of good *intent.ions* or bad *intent.ions* when you have interacted with other people, or even walking into a room you can feel the energy of the people already there.

Our vibes can also sync with people we meet. Have you ever met someone for the first time and felt like you just knew them already somehow? Like the story above, meeting strangers that seemed I had known forever. We've all experienced something like that, both with people we don't know and situations with people we already know.

When I moved back home from Florida, I ran into an old friend, Johnny. The moment I saw him, a shift happened inside me, something that I can't explain. I went home that night and wrote in my journal that I knew Johnny would play an important role in my life. I was sure he came into my circle to teach me things that were vital. But I also had this gut feeling and wrote in my journal that he would only be in my life for a short time.

A few months later Johnny was hit by a drunk driver and killed. There have been numerous times in my life where I had a coincidence that relates back to Johnny. In fact, as I was working on this chapter, Johnny popped into my mind. I unearthed my journal from 1993, and opened it—to exactly the page where I ran into Johnny. His vibration was so powerful, and still is to this very day. He had a profound impact on my life in the short period of time he was here on earth.

We can all have a big impact on the people around us, and it's your choice what your impact will be. I can't think of a better time than now for all of us to plan a strategy to change our vibes into *intent.ional* vibes that emit more positivity, kindness, and compassion. We're in a time of transition and reflection right now, a time that will be in the history books, and how you choose to perceive this time frame of life will either make or break you, as well as those around you.

> If you've ever wanted to be a hero, to make a difference in your community, now is your time to shine your inner light.

You might think "hero" sounds too dramatic, but it's not. Every single one of us has the capacity to effect change in us, around us, and globally. We can be part of birthing a new world of love, compassion, equality, freedom, and oneness by choosing to leave behind thousands of years of corruption, deception, lies, greed, lust, evil, control, and selling our souls for the almighty dollar. As you read this book, I'd like you to see the world we live in with new *eYes* because changing your perception and fine-tuning your vibe is the way we can all develop an unbeatable strategy together.

Choose Your Game Piece Carefully

When you are going through the Game of Life, you pick your Game piece (the character role that you are choosing to play). Be mindful of this title because it will have a huge impact on your vibe. We talked about titles earlier in the Overview section. Choosing which Game piece to play is all about looking inside yourself and seeing what image you are sending the world about who you are. If you aren't that person now, think about what image of yourself you would you like to become. Someone who helps others in delightful and fun ways? Someone slow to judge and fast to forgive? Are you athletic, fit, a gardener, jet-setter, or traveler?

Science has shown that visualization (or imagining our greatest possibilities and outcomes) actually stimulates different regions of our brains because when we visualize an *act.ion* it increases our ability to perform that *act.ion*. We are also able to do it in record time, with increased flexibility, and with more confidence. Athletes use visualization to aid them in breaking records all the time by feeling, seeing, and trusting the desired outcome will happen just as they imagine. It's a mental practice to make the act so familiar that it becomes natural to achieve. Start utilizing this tool today and enjoy the outcome. For more information on this, Google the article by Srinivasan Pillay that ran in the Huff Post on November 17, 2011.

Don't just choose a Game piece/title, go a little further and truly *imagine* yourself in this role. How does this vision of you act? What do you wear, what do you eat, what do you do for work, fun, hobbies, who are your friends and what do they do, where do you travel, etc.? See it, feel it, live it, and talk the talk of that role. You may not be that person yet, but the more you act like that Game piece and visualize (with feeling) your life as that Game piece, the closer you get to actually becoming that person. It's like the old saying of "fake it until you make it."

With every situation you find yourself in, take a moment to imagine how your Game piece would respond or act. The more you perform that role in your mind's imagination, the more ingrained it becomes in yourself, until eventually you are no longer a person with a quick temper or codependent patterns, for example. Instead, you have become someone who responds with the traits you desire, such as courage, integrity, humor, and humility.

> At the end of the day, no matter what Game piece you
> are choosing to play, you are always accountable for all
> your *act.ions* and *re.act.ions*, both to yourself and others.

The role you desire to play should be a constant and *intent.ional* running thought in your head throughout the day. **As soon as you open your *eYes* at the start of the day**, **take a moment to do that visualization exercise, truly seeing yourself as this Game piece.**

Have fun with who you want to become because you can change that person anytime you want, if you desire the change enough. If you get stressed or life throws you a curveball, come back to that image you had in your head at the beginning of the day. As you find your purpose and life mission, you can change or level up your Game piece, so continue to work on yourself to be your best version in all areas of your life.

Choose to Play and Level Up

You're going to face obstacles and challenges as you move along in the Game of Life, trying to reach the next level or achieve the next milestone. Every time that happens, you have the choice to sit out a round or get in there and play. If you keep making the same mistakes, you will continue ending up in the same place—never growing or changing. You'll be the one still sitting on the bench and watching life go by.

Snap out of it—literally! Too many of us end up going through the motions, with the same moves, same decisions, and the *same outcomes*. We take the same route to work every day, have the same breakfast every day, hang out with the same friends, punch in and punch out, over and over, ad nauseum. Do you know someone like this? They live in Pluto's cave, afraid to venture out of the known, but they can also choose to break free.

If you're always asking, *Why is this happening to me again?* I have news for you—it's happening again because you aren't making a *conscious decision* to go in a different direction and to shake up the way you do things. If you don't want to play the same level, you have to approach the Game with a different strategy.

> "The Universe is not pushing you or blessing you with Karma. The Universe is *responding to the vibrational energy* you are sending out. Be mindful of what you *bring into existence.*" —Abraham Hicks

We all have so much power that we aren't tapping into, right inside ourselves. You have the ability to go within to, heal your history, build your inner strength (remove limiting *be.LIE.fs*), and then have faith as you tap more and more into the power of you. Once you realize that you are the one in control and that you can plan your own strategy, it's like an inner-knowing inside because a spark of light ignites inside of you and makes you realize that you are a superhero. **You can change the outcome of this hour, this day, and this life.**

Think of it this way: every time you walk into a different room, you are in a different place in the Game. You have a new opportunity to perceive this space and this moment, with love, and to then create a shift in your perception. You also have a new opportunity to take *intent.ional act.ion* to be the change you want to see in your world. Are you going to run from a challenge? Or are you going to welcome it? Even if you stumble, that's an opportunity to learn and choose differently the next time.

All of the choices you make, from who you choose to be around, your environment, the foods you eat, what you read, what you watch on *tell.A.vision*, all these are things that you can do with *intent.ion*—or you can let someone else (society) do the choosing for you.

When we don't choose, we let society move us around the board. We are influenced by others' decisions instead of making our own. It's like handing over the controller to your opponent in an Xbox game and telling them to play your turn. They aren't going to make the best decisions for you—only *you* can do that.

It's all one step at a time. Make one good decision, and then keep making better decisions over and over again. As you do, you change your vibe and impact your world. Repetition is what allows us to learn and evolve with a deeper *inner-standing*. This works just as it did when you were in school and learned to add and subtract before you evolved and learned to multiply and divide. Eventually you get to the point where those arithmetic lessons are second nature and you can calculate things in your head, just as driving a car became after you did it many times.

Find the Lessons in the Good and the Bad Moments

We learn from both our successes and our failures. After we make the same mistake over and over again, we learn not to touch the hot stove and to use an oven mitt instead (or at least hopefully you learned that!). Some people keep dating the same bad boy/girl or complaining about their job without realizing they have the choice to leave at any time. Stop complaining and either accept it (thereby sitting out your turn) or change the situation (moving forward on the board) because you have the power to be more. You can look at these moments as a gift and an opportunity to evolve.

You will face tough times, maybe even circumstances that seem impossible. All of us have at some point or another. There is no experience you will have that someone else has not had in a similar way. Embrace the challenge, then breathe through it. As you do, feel the *e.motions* inside you shifting and then release them. These key lessons, once you learn to overcome the obstacle, teach you and the others around you.

Think about it like the life-giving water we drink all day. If we held all of that in our bladders, it would be extremely unhealthy and damaging to our bodies. By choosing to release the water when we use the bathroom, we make a healthy choice and make room in our bodies for a new drink. Go with the flow.

> You have to literally piss the crap in your life out and let it go because holding on to it will cause the vibration flow to stop which can cause *dis.ease*.

I get it that this won't be easy and you won't always *re.member* to take the right steps when life throws you a painful detour. I know that when something really horrible happens, like a loved one dies, it's like having the wind knocked out of you. I have personally lost many people in my life. Each loss was a lesson of its own and took time to heal and see differently before I could get my flow back.

If you want to get started with developing a new strategy for yourself, you have to begin with shifting your *e.motions* and how you perceive things. Here are some questions you can ask yourself to help you shift your perception.

1. Is this feeling of depression/abandonment/ unworthiness/unloved/fear/sickness (or whatever) true?

2. Can I see how these feelings/experiences might help me learn, evolve, or transform?

3. Can I see this situation with a loving outcome? (Don't question whether that is possible because everything is possible.)

4. Can I find gratitude in this moment?

5. Can I release the negative feelings and replace them with positive ones?

Letting go allows energy to flow just as a river does into an ocean. Our ocean is the collective consciousness of all, which means you aren't going at it all alone.

Re.member, every situation is as easy or difficult as you **perceive** it to be.

Life Isn't Hard

We are taught from early childhood that life is hard and then you die. Yes, life is hard *if* you cast a spell with your words and tell yourself it's hard (*re.member*, your subconscious is always listening and imprinting). Stop saying life is hard. Replace those words with *life is a challenge and life is beautiful. I have the power to create whatever I desire.*

Spend time every day creating, with conscious imagination, the future you desire. As you do, give thanks and begin to develop a strategy to achieve that life. Start listening to your inner guidance system and intuition to see measurable results. You will shift from floating through life with no real direction to living with empowerment.

When you practice visualization with breathing and observing exercises you are reprogramming your nervous, hormonal, and immune systems. These systems work inside us every day, so why not give them direction for creating the life you desire by being mindfully observant? Done daily, this practice will create a new baseline in your internal systems. Even sixty seconds of visualizing and breathing in a coherent state helps to harmonize your body, mind, and spirit. Imagine what ten minutes or more will do!

For example, if you want a house that belongs to someone else, you don't have to ask the Universe for that exact home. Instead ask and manifest the perfect home for you and your family that is *like* the one you love. Imagine the parts of the home that you love and then feel and see yourself sitting or cooking in those spaces. This allows you to find the home that is right that might even have other features you love more than the original house you adored. Or maybe that home will go on the market because the owners will be moving to a new home that is more perfect for them. See the doors that close as opportunities to open new doors, maybe unexpectedly more pleasing doors.

It's the same with scary events in our lives. Every single time we face a fear, we realize in hindsight that it was not as horrific as we imagined it to be. Think about it—have you faced a fear and afterward said, "Why did I wait so long to do that?" That's how these changes work, too. You alone have the power to create a different version of yourself, a version that is powerful beyond what you ever thought possible.

When you are creating your new strategy for the Game of Life, you essentially stop seeing yourself as the person who is currently in an unhealthy situation, a bad job, or an undesirable neighborhood, but rather visualize yourself as the one who is living your best life.

Gauge your *e.motions* and your *act.ions*. Are you happy every day? Are you feeling fulfilled in your purpose? Are you doing meditation, yoga, or running or whatever motivates you? Are you helping others? As situations present themselves to you, do you *re.act* immediately or do you *pause* and take the time to breathe so that you can respond with love?

That pause is so vital. When you pause and breathe, you can literally feel your intuition guiding you with the right thoughts, feelings, and *act.ions*. Your intuition has been there all along, waiting for you to allow it to create an unbeatable strategy. Trust that internal nudge. It's your compass toward a better life.

THE TRUTH YOU SHOULD KNOW

Society keeps people in a hypnotic state of going through the motions of life in a pattern that becomes comfortable. People don't change because they *don't know there is a way to change*. The truth is that people do change, all the time in many ways, because they choose to do so. The key is in getting comfortable with being uncomfortable and make that your new comfort zone.

When you fall back into your old patterns (which we all do and we know it well so it's easy to do) like eating crappy food because you like the taste, you literally have to stop and tell yourself it tastes awful. Imagine that chip (or whatever) with all the harmful chemicals used to make it. Now, do you want to eat that chip or have some fresh fruit? Or maybe you've been binging on *tell.A.vision* because it's hard to change and you want to watch that new show everyone is talking about. **Stop**. That is a slave mentality (something that is explained at the end of Chapter 7) to do as you are told and be like all the others. Instead, be the change you desire to see.

YOUR DASH ACT.ION

A fun strategy to practice is playing Opposite Day/ Week. When you do this, you use your non-dominant hand to pour your drink, brush your teeth/hair, zip your pants, open doors, turn on lights, etc. By using the opposite arm/hand, this helps your mind make a SHIFT. It sends a message to your brain to perceive things differently.

Also try wearing your watch on the opposite arm (see how many days it takes you to realize you have it on). I did this and for several days never looked at my right arm for my watch (I normally wear it on my left arm). I kept thinking I didn't have my watch on. This exercise trains your mind to perceive everyday things with a new perspective. Create a shift inside you today and have some fun.

THE GUITAR
STRING EXERCISE

Picture a guitar string. The string on its own is just a string (thoughts). The tuning keys (*act.ions*) and volume tone controls (*e.motions*) are nothing without the string between them. But when they are all connected, the melody of sound goes from the string to the tone control to the tuning key, and in between, a wonderful sound is made. To get a better sound from the guitar, you have to tune the strings. It's the same with tuning your life by practicing the Dash Act.ions.

In your life, the volume tone controls on one end are your **e.motions**, pulled from past experiences and *be.LIE.fs*. At the other end, you have the tuning key of **act.ions**, creating your future outcomes. The string between these two are the **thoughts** you are creating. Fine-tune your thoughts with intention and they will vibrate through to create *e.motions* (thereby healing your past) and create the *act.ions* (outcomes) that fit that frequency. You can learn to tune your desired outcomes by shifting your thoughts, *e.motions*, and *act.ions*. Play that music loud when you do!

A thought on its own is nothing without the emotional feeling and the energy that goes throughout your body to create the *act.ion*. When you listen to your intuition and choose to change your vibe, it's as if your strings are all in tune and everything is playing perfectly. This tuning process plays a huge role in your performance/outcome in the Game of Life. Practicing regularly gives you the ability to quickly and easily adjust the string (your thoughts), creating more joy and obtaining your desired outcomes.

Re.member it like a guitar scale:

E: *e.motion s*

A: attract (your)

D: desires (and)

G: gratitude

B: brings

High E: enlightenment

CONTROL YOUR THOUGHTS

On Level 2, we dive deeper into ways you can level up, change how you play the game, and in turn, the way your life evolves. It's all about seeing the power you already have in your heart to change everything.

CHAPTER 4

CHANGE THE GAME BY BREAKING THE CHAINS

"For we wrestle not against flesh and blood, but against principalities against powers, against the rulers of the darkness of this world, against spiritual wickedness in high places."

EPHESIANS 6:12, KJV

When I was a little girl, my dad took me to the St. Louis Zoo. We walked through the exhibits and when we reached the space with the elephants (which was a very small area at that time; it has since been expanded), I saw that the elephant had a chain on his front right leg. We watched this poor elephant sway back and forth, over and over again. My dad, in a dramatic deep voice, said, "Look at that! It's incredible!"

I stared at the elephant, wondering what was so "incredible" about an elephant who was chained in place. My father explained that every time the elephant took a step forward, the chain tugged on his foot. The elephant felt that tug, and this would cause the *re.act.ion* (*act.ion*) of swaying back and forth. In other words, staying in place. To my dad, the incredible part was the mind control the chain had over the elephant. The giant animal had the power within him to pull down a tree, and he had the power to easily break that small chain on his leg, yet because he felt a tug every time he tried to shake it loose, his mind told him he was powerless. That created thoughts of limitation in the elephant—causing the endlessly repeated back and forth movement.

That tug caused a shift in the elephant's brain that created a *be.LIE.f* of limitations, which led to the *act.ion* of swaying instead of using his force to break the cycle. The moral of this story is simple: we are all told and sold limiting thoughts via society, those around us, the media, *tel.LIE.vision*, or our own previous experiences, and those thoughts prevent us from creating the *e.motions* and *act.ions* necessary to break the chain on our minds.

A lot of us accept things in our environment and society and don't question how the world is because we don't *know* to question it, as we talked about earlier. We are afraid to question authority (or what the *ill.u.sion* of our minds perceives as authority). Along the way, we see that for some who do question the status quo, the price they pay is too high. They are shamed, humiliated, cast out by society, so they go back to where they were, much like the elephant (perhaps the elephant in the zoo saw another elephant try to break free from the chain and fail, so he told himself it was futile to even try). That fear prevents us from taking risks, from being all we can be, and from living our best lives.

But what would happen if more people questioned the way the world worked? A ripple effect would take hold and the world would begin to change.

Where in your life do you have the power to easily accomplish your desires but instead, you feel a tug and let it stop you?

We are powerful beyond our imagination, and we can do much more than society has led us to *be.LIE.ve*. The power inside us is there, just waiting to be discovered—but the chains on our mind stop us over and over again.

Fear creates limitations and puts a veil over your thoughts, *e.motions* and *act.ions*. If you pull back the veil and do something you fear, each time it gets easier and you become braver. You overcome your fears and begin to realize you are limitless, and the only thing holding you back is your *be.LIE.f* and mindset.

In the Game of Life, you can become a real-life hero by having the courage to shift your thoughts, and then start to turn the wheel of life in the direction of your inner desires, like the elephant yanking the chain out of the ground and wandering off in a new direction, maybe toward greener pastures. Pull up that heavy anchor that is holding you back so that you can embark on new adventures. Let the journey of a fun-filled, purposeful life begin. Holding on to the past is hurting you, holding you back like those heavy chains. **Stop. Let it go** and **move forward.**

MENTAL CHAINS =
LIMITATIONS & FEAR

In many parts of the world, people are living in poverty. They are living in homes with dirt floors, outdoor showers, and rampant food scarcity. This bears the question: why are these people, who are clearly living lives of despair, not overthrowing their government? After all, the population is huge, much larger than any governmental force. Sadly, many of these people have never known freedom. They don't know what it looks like or feels like. If you've never known something different, then to you, this is how you live and you accept it as your reality.

These people have collectively inherited a mental chain, essentially, around their minds and their thoughts about what their lives could be. They are not able to visualize freedom; it's a foreign concept to them. It's the same with the elephant. If the elephant saw other elephants breaking the chain and walking away, he would be encouraged to realize he could, too. If the people of these poverty-stricken countries saw others overthrowing their government and creating a life of abundance for all, they might be inspired to create the *act.ions* necessary to make that vision happen for them, too.

Think about the Game piece you desire to be, remove any limiting *be.LIE.f* around it, and break the chains holding you in place right now. If someone has done something before that you desire to have or be, then that is evidence and proof it can be done. Likewise, if it has not been done, you can be the leader and show others the path forward.

You have to know in your heart that you can achieve—and have—a life of definite purpose. You *can* have all that you desire. This is happening as you read this. People are standing up and taking *act.ion*. If you choose to be willing to change and trust that you can escape those chains and have the life of purpose, it will change the way you play. I like to call this another Game Changer!!!

The Influence of Society— The Elephant in the Room

Those chains are also found in the people around us and their influences. We have been conditioned by society to obey, to follow orders, and to trust the media and authority (which, in reality, are our equals). When we see something wrong, society teaches us *not* to ask the Captain Obvious question of "What is going on here? Why is that poison in our water/food necessary?

Isn't it harmful?" We look the other way, refusing to see that elephant standing in front of us.

We don't ask these questions because we are so busy doing our own thing, we don't have time or know the method to ask questions, plus we don't realize the difference we could make. We are unknowingly giving our power over to another. That is done on purpose by society, to control outcomes and take freedoms away gradually so it goes unnoticed and we stay silent. Silence is, in essence, consent.

It is time we all **STOP**, and realize that this is the most *incredible* moment in time to be alive. We are at a turning point in this Game of Life. We have the power, opportunity, and privilege to change the course of this Game and to become the pioneers of a revolutionary new Game of Life.

You get behind the wheel in the Game by taking simple *act.ions* like sending emails or calling people like elected officials, heads of corporations, agencies, etc. You begin questioning everyone about everything. This is simple and easy to do, so let's make it a new normal. Ask questions like: "Why are there chemicals in our water and food?" "Why do we have to do things this way?" "Why are we not changing this?" "Why are we not teaching kids critical thinking and hands-on learning?" "Why are elected officials, corporations, and others not promoting natural cures?" "If the natural treatments are just as effective, why is insurance not covering those?"

When you question the way things are done, the vibration inside of you increases and your light shines brighter. We each have a duty to make one another accountable for the *act.ions* being taken in the title roles that are being played. We are all tasked with rewarding good and punishing the evildoers in order to mirror the justice and laws of God in the Game of Life. Accountability is required for all players, at all times, which is why we ask questions.

The Game of Life is at a pivotal point, and you are here with a purpose, mission, and reason: to break the chains on yourself and society. You've got this.

> Think of it this way: society's mission is to help us evolve our consciousness. Society does evil things openly to give us the opportunity to level up by calling them out. Be Toto, pull back that veil. Step into your true power. This is the Law of Inspired Act.ion at play.

For example, maybe you found out that a new law is harmful and is about to be voted on by your representatives. Do you call or send an email? Or do you feel powerless to do anything about it? Maybe it seems like too big of a mountain to climb and you aren't the right person to climb it. Society has conditioned us to *be.LIE.ve* the lie that we are helpless. We feel paralyzed and clueless about what we could do that would change the outcome. That is hogwash, it's a trap, we are supposed to take *act.ion*. Society is waiting for us to level up this Game. Plus, these kinds of *act.ions* instill the feeling of **empowerment inside** you and the people around you. You set a vibe when you take these *act.ions*, one that is felt by the collective consciousness of those in your community. Don't underestimate your abilities; you are a **hero** in this Game. Break the chains on your mind and see that elephant in the room.

Take the Reins

Too often, we have been made to feel foolish for calling our representatives or writing emails to people in government. Maybe nothing on the surface changed or you told a friend about your call or email and they laughed. Or maybe you're just thinking your voice isn't worth anything. You might be thinking, *Who am I to question fictious authority?*

I say: **Who are you NOT to question them?** Maybe you work for a company that is doing things that are wrong, like dumping toxic waste into a river, but you hesitate to speak up because of your pension or your wages (money is a trap to control you and keep you at a low vibe). No job is worth giving up your morals, ethics, or principals. Plus, they only get away with these unethical *act.ions* because no one questions them. Once one person stands up, many will follow. There are always other jobs and better careers out there. You could even start your own business.

It's worth it, for the good of all, to speak up and start that shift for the world. Personal empowerment comes when we each start to question the false authority of bosses/teachers/board members/government officials/media, and the others around us, but always with a heart of compassion (that is key).

Questioning the people who put the chains in place, even if they had the best of *intent.ions* at the time, helps us begin to break the chains holding us in place. I write emails to people in power all the time. I've seen bills removed from the floor or not passed after I've written a letter. Was it my email that changed a vote or decision? Maybe, maybe not. But I know I am taking the *act.ions* that will help this world, rather than idly sitting by. And that, my friend, is setting a vibe that is felt in the collective consciousness of all.

Re.member The Law of Oneness that we talked about in the first chapter? We are all, essentially, from the same source. Each person is a part of the whole that connects us all. Calling out a person doing a wrong helps save the person doing it, by giving them the chance to repent (to see the error of their ways). You are essentially setting into motion the vibe to help them raise up their own vibe. It's a win for all.

You are responsible for your own thoughts and for choosing to set yourself free. In doing so, you show others the pathway to freedom. Choose to ask questions, to take risks, and to perceive the Game differently. It is our responsibility to create a new life for ourselves and mankind. One of love, joy, compassion, freedom, and rock 'n roll.

Ask yourself: What is binding me to these old *be.LIE.fs*?

When you create the shift in your thoughts, you are *choosing* to respond versus *re.act*, which creates internal changes. You will become someone who has a deeper *inner.standing* of how things work and that encourages others to do the same.

If you want to inner-stand more, start your journey to discover your own truth. Are you open to changing your *be.LIE.fs* based on new findings? When you are open to thinking in new ways, you raise your consciousness and your vibration. Are you willing to detach from your *be.LIE.fs*? Sometimes this journey of discovery might feel like you jumped into ice-cold water and you have to catch your breath. You'll be fine, the water (your crumbling *be.LIE.fs*) gets warmer each time you jump in. It's actually the funnest part of the Game.

Here's the truth: **You already have the power to break your own mental chains.** Here are a few ways to begin doing that:

- **Know You Can Do It:** We have been programmed to *be.LIE.ve* we are powerless and have limits to our abilities. As schoolchildren, we are taught to obey and not taught to think critically or to ask questions. Stop that line of thinking and break free by questioning the man-made laws and teachings that are holding us back. Our abilities are indeed powerful beyond our imagination and each of us, like the elephant, has far more power than we realize.

- **Choose the People Around You:** When you are in a group, it creates a collective conscience, or a vibe. It's important to be around like-minded people who bring positivity, not negativity, to your life. Don't cling to bad, dead-end relationships. Let go of those not serving your greatest, highest self. That *act.ion* might help to create a change in a friend or create a new and better friendship in return.

- **You Don't Need Other People's Approval:** I used to want other people's approval. To fit in. That constant quest for other people to rubberstamp approval on what you do and say is part of the deception and lies that trap you in the quicksand. When you are always looking outside yourself for validation, it creates a low and negative vibe inside you. Instead, seek from within.

As I started to shift my thinking and go within for guidance (trusting my heart), I began to perceive the world differently and stopped caring what others thought, especially if it meant I had to compromise my truth. Break those chains that are holding you back from your best life! It's liberating.

THE TRUTH YOU SHOULD KNOW

Society pressures us to do as we're told, fit in, and conform to the rules; otherwise, you're crazy and people will talk about you and shame you. That is why we are in the current state of the world—because everyone desperately wants to conform and fit in, be liked, not stand out. This is a slave mindset because it affects how you see yourself. It prevents you from seeing yourself the way God sees you. You feel the constant need to depend on someone or something outside of you.

That must end.

Say out loud:

"I was not born to fit in; I was born to stand out!!!!"

Be okay with being the leader because that is what it takes to shift you and the world. It's the premise of the Game of Life.

YOUR DASH ACT.ION

To change the Game, you have to change your thinking and question your *be.LIE.fs*. Start by being an observer of yourself and detach from the outcome/situation and *be.LIE.f* you hold. Are you serving your highest and best self? Or are you staying stuck in old patterns and behaviors? Break one chain this week, whether that is outdated thinking, an irrational fear, or a bad habit you have fallen back on as a crutch. Start an *act.ion* step on whatever you are passionate to change and notice the shift inside you and how much freer you feel.

USING THE
FOUR ELEMENTS

Land/Earth: Get into nature every day, go barefoot on the grass, take a walk (with no electronics). These *act.ions* help you ground and center your soul , mind, and body, and align with the electromagnetic field of Mother Earth.

Air: Breathe in life. *Dis.ease* does not happen in a body that is alkaline and oxidized. Breathe mindfully to calm yourself. We often hold our breath when we are stressed, fearful, anxious, or mad. *Re.member* to breathe!!!

Water: This is your life-force energy. Drink a gallon of clean, chemical-free water daily; it gives you energy and washes out *dis.ease*. Take a salt bath for clarity. It helps to holistically clean your body, spirit, and mind.

Fire: This is your heart's burning desire and passion to follow your purpose; it's what motivates you to be all you can be. Listen to it.

CHAPTER 5

LEVEL UP WITH AN INTENT.IONAL SHIFT

"Our deepest fear is not that we are inadequate. Our deepest fear is that we are powerful beyond measure. It is our light, not our darkness, that most frightens us. We ask ourselves, who am I to be brilliant, gorgeous, talented and fabulous? Actually, who are you not to be? You are a child of God. Your playing small does not serve the world."

MARIANNE WILLIAMSON
EXCERPT FROM *A RETURN TO LOVE*

At the same time I was beginning my journey with the concept of using my thoughts to live my best, most-abundant life, a friend and I enrolled in a class on setting *intent.ions*. The whole idea of simply setting an intention and then watching it come true seemed impossible to me. But I decided to test this theory and give it a go.

I desired a larger salary at the time, so I set my *intent.ions* on getting a 25% increase in what I was being paid and getting that done by the middle of the year. A few weeks later, I was at work when I received a call from a company asking me if I would be interested in coming in for an interview. I had not applied for a job anywhere; the CEO received my name from an associate I work with and he thought I would be a good fit for the company. (Fun fact: this was before the internet made that kind of thing easy.)

I had nothing to lose and went for the interview. The job seemed perfect. It was closer to home and everyone who worked there seemed nice. The type of work was something I had never done before but I was confident I could learn. They offered me 15% more than I was making, which was great, but I really wanted that 25% increase. The next day, I asked my current boss if we could chat. I told him I had been offered a position and would be leaving. At the end of the conversation, I suggested to him a position and job description that I created the night before for something that was needed within the company. Mind you, I would not have been so bold normally, but I was leaving for another company and figured I had nothing to lose. My boss thought the job idea was great. He asked me to stay on at the company and told me that "maybe" they would create this position down the road.

I wasn't willing to wait on a maybe so I left. I started my new role at the other company and loved it. A few months after I started, my old boss called me up and asked if we could talk. He told me he had created the job that I gave him, but the only person he thought was perfect for it was me. He offered me a 25% bump in the salary I had been making. Again, being bold, I asked for a sign-on bonus—and got it.

As I left my new job, I felt bad about quitting. I gave them the name of a friend who would be perfect for the position. They hired her and ten years later, she ended up hiring me to come back there to work. By that time, my salary was much higher than the original 25% I had set my sights on.

The miracle of setting your *intent.ions* is found in doing so with a good heart, and most importantly, having the trust and the faith that it will transpire. You don't need to know by what means or even entertain all those questions about how it will happen. Set your *intent.ions* (i.e., your thoughts), start being mindful (aware) of opportunities that come, and be willing and ready to take the *act.ion* steps—then be prepared for that change, that transformation, to materialize.

Shift the Thinking, Set the Intention

We set *intent.ions* all day, every day, mindfully or not. The act of starting your day by either getting out of bed or hitting the alarm is a determination. You either purposely choose to sleep longer (snooze and lose) or get up and dash into *act.ion*. Intention, then, is just another word for purpose. So many of us are looking for purpose outside of ourselves, completely unaware that our purpose is found in our inner desires.

Intention setting isn't complicated, but it can be a challenge for many of us to turn off that part of the brain that is full of mental roadblocks and limiting thoughts about why something can't happen. Once you learn how to set your *intent.ions*/purpose, you begin to level up in the Game of Life quickly.

Think about the word intent.ions:

"Intent" = a desire + "ions" = "the act.ion of" or "the result of."

Intent.ions = a purpose, aim, goal or desire + ions = an electric charge which creates the result. Essentially, your desire or purpose creates the results you see.

I bet you have already set *intent.ions* many times without even realizing you achieved them. You may have set your mind's *eYe* on something you wanted and when you received it, you may have shrugged it off because of how easy it was to accomplish. Maybe you got an A on a test or a reward at work and thought "no biggie" because you put the effort into it and assumed it would happen.

It is said that you are whatever your mind can conceive of and accept as true. **Your mind is POWER**. Ask yourself: *What am I capable of attaining, achieving, accomplishing if I set intention on a desired outcome? Can you conceive this happening?*

Think of people in history or your life who have made an impact that brought about change. One person's *act.ions* can cause a tidal wave of transformation.

With smaller goals, setting *intent.ions* is easy. Going after our deep-down desires is where we often get stuck because in our mind these desires are a BIG DEAL and therefore, impossible to attain. Learn to trust in the power of intention and stop playing small in order to move forward to the next level.

Everything you desire can be achieved. When you trust in the power of intent with imagination, you are breaking a chain that might have held you back in the past. You are also setting the stage, not just for yourself, but for others who desire similar achievements. You are blazing a path by showing those around you how to break those restricting thoughts of limitation, fear, doubt, and being unworthy.

Stop Playing Small

Setting your *intent.ions* is just the beginning. You must set the wheels in motion by first visualizing your life as if you have already accomplished your purpose (like getting an A on the test, see it as a done deal). For example, I've wanted to write a book ever since I was in second grade. I've kept journals all my life and in every single one of them I mention the books I will write. Years go by and in that time, I've told all my friends about my wish to write a book. But no book comes about because all this time, I was just talking about it. That made it a wishful dream with no *act.ion* plan.

Then I took one tiny step forward and looked at websites that talked about how to write a book, but I was soon lost in all the information because I had no clear drive, no *act.ion* plan, no resolve. In short, I didn't perceive it as a done deal.

In my mind, I was thinking, *Who am I to write a book?* In other words, I was playing small. My insecurities held me back from having confidence in myself and that lack of confidence (in my thoughts) kept me from acting.

Still, I felt this inner, burning desire to be more, do more, have more, and to feel alive inside. Despite that desire, every evening for years on end, instead of working on my book, I watched *tell.A.vision.* I was bored out of my mind and felt worthless because I was not going after my purpose. I was literally sitting there on the couch, mentally chained to where I sat. Have you done this? Can you relate to what I was going through? Chances are, you can.

I always thought writing a book was something *other* people did. I would think, *I'm not an author.* When I kept saying that to myself, I was casting a spell that would make sure I wasn't an author. So, I replaced that thought with "I *am* an author" and I kept repeating it to myself over and over again. I started walking through bookstores and imagining my book on the shelves, picturing where it would be located, what my cover would look like. I imagined people coming up to me to get my autograph. I set my thoughts into e.motion to perceive the outcome I desired.

Be mindful because a lack of intention brings on unwanted results. Whenever you say something negative about yourself or negative about anything else, immediately say, either mentally or aloud: "Cancel/ Clear" or "Erase." These two phrases come in handy to remove that low thought vibration and replace it with a positive vibe instead.

The limitations that I put on myself in my own mind were that I wasn't good enough and I wasn't worthy. I kept thinking *I need this* or *I need that* before I can get started. I *unintent.iona*lly attracted lack with those thoughts. Every day that passed without me taking *intent.ional act.ion*, I was giving those thoughts some credibility and allowing them to take root even deeper. Pull that root out of your brain as if it's a weed and get rid of it.

One hot summer day, I was watering my plants and listening to Joe Vittel's audio book, *The Abundance Paradigm*. His words began to speak to me and right there in the yard, something shifted in me mentally. I stopped watering the plants, ran inside, and began writing down the way I desired my life to be and the person I anticipated to be. Most of all, I began to feel like I *deserved* that life and deserved to be that person.

That mental shift, coupled with that first *act.ion* step, set into motion an instant change. Right after I wrote all these things down, my friend Andrea called me, asking if I wanted to go out to lunch. We hadn't gone to lunch in years, and her timing was incredible and clearly part of the Universe at work. While we were at lunch, Andrea told me about her life coach, Laura, and how working with Laura had transformed her life. I asked Andrea to connect me, and I immediately called Laura.

Soon after I start working with Laura, there was an earthquake-sized shift inside me that woke up my soul. Mind you, I have been on and off the "spiritual train" my entire life, but for a long time I was derailed. Nevertheless, my soul longed to be connected to my inner guidance and power again. Laura and I discussed some of the things I had a passion inside me to accomplish, and in the process, I began another new journey toward self-discovery and finding my purpose. One spark of an idea lead to more, like a tidal wave. This is the result of going with the flow of intention.

You must have conviction with your intention(s) and perceive that they have power.

However, I still felt like I was missing something. When I talked to Andrea again, I thanked her for introducing me to Laura. Then I asked her if she knew of any groups or programs that offered a combination of workouts, meditation/breathing, and healthy eating with accountability. The kind of program that would kick my butt if I didn't do the work. "Yes," she said. "I have the perfect program for you to look into. Look up Katie Boyd."

Katie Boyd was offering a program that was on-point with everything I was looking for. She brought together meditation, yoga, eating healthy, walking daily, journaling, and setting *intent.ions*, along with accountability calls and advice on moving forward and becoming my highest, best self. I knew right then that Katie, whom I now call my friend, was someone who was going to kick my butt and not let me play small. Katie showed me how to shift my mindset and step into my true power by going within and challenging all my core *be.LIE.fs* at a much deeper level than I had ever experienced. Imagine being on a ride that shakes your whole body with tremendous force and afterward you still feel that vibration sensation—that is the level of awakening that I experienced.

For example, my relationship with food changed. Instead of eating junk, I paused and questioned, "Is that really for my highest, best self? Do I really want to eat this? Am I eating because I am bored or because I am hungry?" What we eat plays a significant role in our life.

I was not able to walk around the block when I started the program (due to an injury), but by the third week I was walking ten thousand steps with no pain because my food choices helped reduce my inflammation. That was just one aspect of her program. I not only achieved my ultimate goals (physically, mentally, and spiritually), I *surpassed* each of them. That is an *intent.ional* shift in the right direction.

Find someone in your life who motivates you to be your highest, best self and in turn, do the same for them. If you don't know someone like that right now, how do you find that person? By setting the intention to find them, imagining the outcome, and anchoring that feeling in your gut.

> Pause for a moment and think of a time someone did or said something that shifted your perspective, or think of a time when you did that for someone else. Just imagine if that was the new normal, where we were all helping each other be our best selves. Start making that world a reality now by choosing to be around others who support you and you return that support.

Listen to Your Gut

The minute I saw Katie's program, something about it resonated inside me. I knew I had to take *act.ion* right then and there. There was no room for hesitation or asking how or why. I acted on my instincts. Katie became a GAME CHANGER (mentally, spiritually, and physically) in my life because here I am, writing my first book, a dream I have desired all my life. I told Katie writing a book was my deep desire, and she helped me define the *act.ion* plan to get me started. It was not by chance these people or circumstances happened; it was the Universe working with me (being in the flow) because of the *intent.ional* vibration I put into motion.

I tell you this story as an example of how setting your desires into motion naturally brings the people into your life that you need when you need them. In setting your desires, trusting that they

will happen, and then taking *intent.ional* steps in that direction, you set the vibration to attract that same vibe, which drives you closer to your desired life.

> Your thoughts and words are more powerful than you realize. You have the power to accomplish whatever you imagine. You can even heal yourself. Edgar Cayce said that treating the physical body without healing the other aspects of the self (the mental, emotional, and spiritual) is like putting a bandage on a blown tire. Whether it's health, finance, relationships, or home—whatever problems you are having will repeat until you go within and heal your consciousness and heart.

Just like changing the channel on your tell.A.vison, you can do the same with your life.

The more I shifted, the stronger my intuition became. I felt alive again. You have to learn to trust those gut feelings. If you are hesitating to take a risk or make a change, ask yourself: *Am I overthinking it? Is this opportunity knocking? Am I going to answer it or ignore it? What is the worst thing that can happen, and if that happens, is it really that bad?*

Learn to take one step after another, even if you can't see the next few steps. Just trust that the Universe is guiding you in the right direction and when you need that next step, it will be there waiting for you. In the movie *A Wrinkle in Time,* Meg Murry is walking upstairs on invisible stairs. The next step doesn't appear until she takes the *act.ion* of trusting it will appear (she can't see the steps with her *eYes*). **That is what this Game of Life is about: trusting you already have everything you need waiting inside you.**

Before I learned to fully trust in the power of my *intent.ions*, my life had slipped into a rut of despair, hopelessness, and boredom. I had achieved the salary goal I intended, but when it came to reaching higher goals, I doubted myself. I was caught in a pattern of going to work, binging Netflix, or having drinks with friends and then going to bed. I wasn't living my best life, or really living at all. I was going through the motions and repeating that day in and day out, like a zombie. I could beat myself up for all that lost time, but I won't. It's important to give yourself grace if you slip off track. Look at those times as a break that you needed, for without that time, you would not be who you are now.

> My struggle was twofold: I needed to challenge myself to trust, and I had to begin watching my self-talk. Instead of saying I can't, I began to say, "Erase," and replace it with "I can" or "I am" and then I started feeling, Why not me?

Be empowered. You are not a drifter, wandering around life helpless. YOU ARE POWERFUL. Start manifesting the change you envision right this second. You don't have to wait until Monday or January 1st. You can do it today, in this moment of time. Set your thoughts with visualization, allow the e.motion to flow to the *act.ion* steps, and trust what comes. Be ready because it will come.

Cultivate that deep passion inside you to do more and be more. There is so much more out there then we are programmed to *be.LIE.ve*. Yep, I said *programmed*. A tel.LIE.vision is programmed and even the channel guide is programmed to suck you into a certain vibe pattern. Your brain is much the same way. You can choose to reprogram the circuitry in your head. Stop watching all those channels that have been created by society, paradigms, and negative self-talk. Pick a new vibe and create your own channel—today. Changing the channel is as simple as the Dash Act.ions herein, where you begin visualizing and becoming the person you are born to be.

That deep desire/passion inside you is your purpose in life. Know that you deserve more and are worthy of your purpose.

That day in the yard, a fire was sparked inside of me to seek direction. Like a miracle, Andrea called, which led me to Laura and Katie. They helped me stoke that fire and the bigger it burned, the more my fear began to flow out of me. Today, I don't fear losing a job or being bold by speaking my truth because the passion inside of me is so strong and fierce. It's a voice I can't ignore. By my *act.ion* of speaking up about what I desired, a portal of opportunities suddenly appeared in the form of like-minded people, programs, situations, and speaking events. When you set your *intent.ions*, the power of your purpose comes alive and is unstoppable.

THE TRUTH YOU SHOULD KNOW

Miracles are happening daily to you, all around you, everywhere. Stop brushing off things that seem like a coincidence and start noticing how often they happen daily. When you set your intention to notice, you will see miracles of all shapes and sizes are abundant around you.

YOUR DASH ACT.ION

Start your day with affirmations of what you desire, visualize (see yourself in that future as if it's now). In essence, create your own personal *tell.A.vision* with your vision and your channels. Put those affirmations around your home to remind you. Say them out loud when you see them. Bring that vision into focus, trust it has already happened, and it will come.

Ask and you shall receive—give thanks for already having it—know all things are possible.

LET GO

We often stay in a low vibe of familiarity because it is comfortable and it seems too hard to change. If I gave you a can of soup right now to hold, you'd think it wasn't heavy. But if you hold it for an hour (never putting it down), how heavy would it seem?

That can of soup is like all the past hurts we hold on to. They weigh us down. Stop holding on to that can of soup so that you can have a lighter, brighter future.

CHAPTER 6

LET YOUR IMAGINATION MAKE THE MOVES

"Logic will get you from A to B.
Imagination will take you everywhere."

ALBERT EINSTEIN (1879-1955)
NOBLE PRIZE–WINNING PHYSICIST

My dad was a storyteller. I *re.member* people gathering around him, on the edges of their seats, waiting to hear how his newest tale would end. We would all hang on his every word. His imagination was electric, his heart pure and strong, and because of that, his stories touched many people.

Sadly, my dad transitioned to heaven over three decades ago. More than a thousand people attended his funeral, packing the entire church on an Easter weekend. Ironically, it was also April 1st, his favorite day, because he loved to play jokes on everyone, especially on April Fool's Day. At the funeral, my uncle gave the eulogy. He had everyone laughing as he talked about the two of them taking a simple trip to the store to get bread which turned into an adventure that my uncle treasured forever.

Even now, thirty years later, people stop me to share stories about my father. It was more than just how he helped them or did something for them. It was how he brightened their lives with his spirt and the **enthusiasm** he had to make everyone feel appreciated, cared for, and most of all, loved. His passion and joy came from his heart, which was why being around him was literally electrifying. He took small and normally meaningless moments and turned them into something special because his imagination was led by his heart. That's why he left such a strong impression long after he was gone.

WHAT WILL YOUR LEGACY BE?

My dad was incredible and left behind a fun, loving legacy. What do you want to be re.membered for? What characteristics do you want people to re.member about you? Write that intention down so you can focus on it and be guided to take act.ions that lead you to that legacy. For me, I want to be like my dad and to be re.membered as someone who had a passionate heart to help inspire others to find their true power.

I wanted to share some of my father's wisdom because he had a way of looking at the world that made me stop and think. That's exactly why I wrote this book for you—to help you stop and think and use your imagination to see things in a new and different way.

Things My Daddy Used to Say:

Study All Religions: My dad told me to study every religion and look for the truth and similarities in all of them. When you do that, you can comprehend the Game of Life at a deeper level of consciousness. It also teaches you to look for the things we have in *common* rather than focusing on our differences, which creates a much more positive and *intent.ional* vibe. Religion can be a divider because people's hard-core *be.LIE.fs* can cause them to seem mean or heartless. But if you learn to look for the common ground, you will open the gateways of mindfulness.

Question Everything and Everyone*:* I moved home during college and even then, my dad would wait up for me to get home. In those quiet hours when the house was asleep, he and I would get into deep discussions about the meaning of life. He encouraged me to question everyone and everything. He explained that if someone gets mad by being questioned, most likely they are hiding something. Otherwise, why would they get upset? Ask them why it's upsetting them. He also said to question everything on *tell.LIE.vision.* My dad always said newspeople are paid actors, playing a role in a Hollywood production (an *ill.u.sion*). Even after he passed away in 1991, I never really watched the news again, and I have become a voracious reader, researching and learning more every day.

Look for the Truth*:* My dad encouraged me to look for truth, to never take something as true just because someone said it, even if that person was someone in authority. Dad's reasoning was that if Santa was a lie (which is where I got that example for Chapter 1), then what else is a lie? Many people will *be.LIE.ve* something just because others *be.LIE.ve* it, without questioning the source or validity. He wanted me to always seek truth, think broader, and to imagine seeing all that is hidden in plain sight.

Many people see things that others don't; it's like two worlds existing within one. As above, so below; as within, so without. Have you ever looked at those pictures with multiple meanings?

I love those, especially the ones with many details. This Game of Life has many hidden in plain sight discoveries and when you awaken your mind's *eYe* (which is your pineal gland), you can see that the world has many marvelous wonders all around us.

Control the Ingredients of Your Intention

My dad was a naturally loving person, but like anyone, he had bad days or days when he was grumpy. However, he was very *intent.ional* about turning around his thoughts so that the vibe he gave off wasn't negative. He wasn't going to share his frustrations and disappointments with others because he wanted to be a positive force in everyone's lives. Before there were dozens of books on the topic, he knew the importance of setting his *intent.ions*.

Setting your *intent.ions* is a lot like making a cake. Whether you want it to be chocolate or vanilla flavored, you have to gather the right ingredients to mix in order to achieve the finished product. Your thoughts are ingredients added together to create the "*intent.ion*" of your mental cake (your *e.motions* are the result of combining those ingredients), and your *act.ions* are what get the cake into the oven and then into your belly. The icing (which you should always have) is your imagination.

With a cake, if your baking powder is outdated, the cake won't rise because one of the ingredients is bad. It works the same with your mental cake. If your *e.motions* are in chaos (bad ingredients) then the outcome is *act.ions* which bring you trauma/sadness/grief (a flat or bad-tasting cake). Maybe that negative outcome is anxiety, trouble breathing, or the inability to think clearly. You might think that's all out of your control, but that's not true.

Just as you control the kind and amount of ingredients in your cake, you can also control the kind and amount of your thoughts. Switch your thoughts by focusing on creating a *response* instead of a *re.act.ion* that just creates a bigger mess. A *re.act.ion* (that instantaneous word or *act.ion* you have right after something happens) often leads to harming yourself or others with your words and *act.ions*. That can fracture relationships and leave a lasting negative image around you.

Think of a time when you *re.act*ed too quickly. Now think about how you would do that moment differently if you took a second to pause before you responded. **You need to change the ingredients in order to change the result.**

When your baking powder goes bad, you don't keep using it and hope it will magically start working. You toss it out and buy a new container. It's the same with your mind. By healing your past traumas (hurt, guilt, sadness, resentment, shame, judgement, etc.) you release those thoughts (the bad ingredients) and replace them with joyful, happy, compassionate, loving, kind thoughts. You're no longer holding on to low vibes in your body, mind, and spirit, and now you have the power of choice to insert good vibes. Sound too good to be true? It's not. It's as simple or as hard as you *be.LIE.ve* it to be.

THE SCIENCE BEHIND RE.ACT.IONS

You've probably heard of fight or flight—that's a re.act. ion that is controlled by an area of the brain referred to as the amygdala. The amygdala is the part of the brain that makes you panic, instantly feel angry, or have the urge to run away. The prefrontal cortex, however, is like a pause button. It allows you to think through your response and act from a place of reason. To put a halt on the amygdala and give your prefrontal cortex a second to kick in, practice breathing (go to HeartMath for some quick and easy techniques). Mindful breathing is the break your brain needs to allow you to control your emotional responses.

Create Better Cellular Memory

The thoughts you have become embedded in your cells; that's why it's so important to release your negative *e.motions* and thoughts. Your body is 70% water, and water holds memory, which means your cells hold memory. In 1994, Japanese researcher Dr. Masaru Emoto did an experiment with water to demonstrate the effect. His water experiment was called The Power of Thoughts. In it, he took photos of water with words written on the glass and noted the crystalline structures they form when the glass contained positive versus negative words. The results are amazing.

Words carry a vibration. In the experiment, *love* and *thank you* showed as soft edges and beautiful shapes, while *fear* and *hate* both had sharp, jagged edges. Think about that for a moment. If you have hateful words or feelings inside you, your body is full of cells with jagged edges (*dis.ease*). Soften it up by thinking, speaking, and imagining words of love throughout the day. Then notice how these words heal and affect your vibe and those of the people around you.

Your body, spirit, and mind want you to move forward in a positive direction and communicate this message to you all the time, in subtle ways. When you keep experiencing the same thing over and over again (a bad relationship, a terrible job, a hurtful friend), it's the Universe's way of telling you, "Enough! Let this go and heal already."

Here's the simple truth: **holding on to pain and not healing your past will cause you to keep *re.act.ing* the same way. If**

you want to escape that vicious circle, you have to heal the past and let it flow out of you. Imagine it breaking apart into small bubbles and floating away, dissolving in a pool of love.

WASH IT AWAY

Often when I am in the shower (in the middle of water), a past event will come to mind. That memory is my mind and soul giving me a nudge to heal the event. I go through my exercises of reimagining the situation with my heart at the center and then visualize all that negativity washing down the drain.

Your imagination is there to help you perceive an amazing future, one where you have let go of all those negative (low vibe) *e.motions* like anger, jealousy, envy, greed, or lust. Close your *eYe*s and imagine a lifestyle that aligns with your goals and is filled with compassion and love. Love is the most powerful vibrational force in our world and using your imagination to nurture it will begin to rewrite your cells and your life. Cast the spell of LOVE onto yourself.

The Movie/Song Imagination Experiment

Let's do a quick fun experiment to identify feelings that come up for you with movies and songs. Both of these art forms are created because of someone else's imagination and in turn, their imagined world and *intent.ions* impact you, both negatively and positively. Songs are quick vibe impactors, while movies trigger

121

a totally different level of your subconscious because they are so immersive. Doing this exercise gives you two options to turn to when you are feeling challenged to have an upbeat vibration. Look for the messages your intuition is sending when you experience movies and songs. When you can see the connection between imagination and thought, it makes it easier to use the power of your mind to affect positive outcomes for yourself and your life.

Think of movie(s) that:

1. Bring tears to your *eYe*s.

    - For me, that movie is *The Notebook* because of the undying love between them and the passion they shared with each other.

2. Make you laugh out loud.

    - For me, it's the comedy *Liar, Liar*. The message I hear when I watch this movie is to always tell that truth, even if it's difficult.

3. Makes you think about life in a different way.

    - I have several of these kinds of movies that I've watched many times. *The Matrix* opened my mind's *eYe* to the matrix of life. *Inception* helped me realize all kinds of things we can create with our imagination. *Hunger Games* shows that our lives are a Game being played right now, as well as the role society plays and our ability to be the heroes in our own lives. *Tomorrow Land,* because the main character refuses to *be.LIE.ve* the future is already determined and knows we do have power to change our destinies. Finally, all the superhero movies because they remind me that we all have super powers of our own.

4. You can watch over and over and never get bored with.

- *It's a Wonderful Life* always reminds me that life is worth living if you just look at it differently, and *Scrooge* because its main message is that you can use the past, present, and future to create a new and better now.

5. Confirm a shift in consciousness or growth happening as you watch them now versus in the past.

- *Jaws* made me so scared that I didn't want to go swimming anywhere. Over time, I overcame that false fear and now laugh at how fake the movie looks. The first *Star Wars* was state-of-the art-when I watched it, but now the world theatrics have changed and you realize how far we have evolved by using technology.

Next, think about songs that:

1. Tug at your heart.

- *Wind Beneath My Wings* by Bette Midler reminds me of those who stand by my side and lift me up.

"Imagine" by John Lennon has helped me imagine a world of love and peace.

2. Take you back in time to a special memory and/or place.

 • *Stairway to Heaven* by Led Zeppelin has always made me *re.member* that there is "still time to change" whatever road you're taking, if you stop following the piper everyone else follows. And *Breakfast in America* by SuperTramp reminds me of my brother Tim playing this loudly on his eight-track player (*re.member* those?). Now, as an adult, I can see all the double meanings and hidden undertones in this song.

3. Lift you up and encourage you to dance and sing out loud.

 • *Footloose* by Kenny Loggins, *Bohemian Rhapsody* by Queen, and *I Feel Good* by James Brown, which is a song I use for my morning alarm so I start the day feeling great and energized.

4. Make you think about life a bit differently.

 • *Man in the Mirror* by Michael Jackson reminds me that change starts with yourself. You can look in the mirror and imagine who you can be and all the good you can do for others. *Crumblin' Down* by John Mellencamp tells me that you can tear down the walls within, as well as the walls in our world.

5. Leave you with a negative vibe.

- I switch the station or play the next track with songs that have a low vibe.

After you have made these lists, go back and look at your life. If your life was a movie or song, how would it play out/sound? What changes would you edit out of or into your life movie/song? Now close your *eYe*s and imagine a new movie/song for your life. What *act.ions* will you take to create that reality?

Imagine Your New World

Whether it's a song or movie, the director/actors/writer started off by imagining what mood they wanted to evoke inside the viewer/listener. They put a great deal of thought into colors, sounds, and words to manifest that outcome. Every detail is used to pull you in and immerse you in a particular feeling or mood. Their imagination affected you and made you feel something that they planned. You have the power to do the same thing with your own mind and *intent.ions*.

I want you to close your *eYe*s, relax, and imagine what the future holds for you. Then get out a notebook and answer these questions. Be as detailed as you can:

- What does your imagined life-movie and life-song feel like to you and those around you?

- What is the state of affairs of the world you are creating? Is it war and drama or heaven on earth? *Re.member*, you are the director.

- What are you willing to do now to help this vision for your life, and for the world, to become a reality?

Regularly revisit your answers and imagine this loving world with intensity. Tweak your answers as you evolve in consciousness and things come to you. It is up to *every single one of us* to build a world of compassion, love, and freedom for all. It starts with doing that for ourselves first.

It is time for us to join together to help our world raise its vibe. Together we will create a world of vitality, but we have a bit of a mess to clean up first. That is not a bad thing; it's an opportunity to shine your light and be a hero. Imagine that world and see the journey of the story unfolding in your mind, all the way up to the happy ending you envisioned.

CREATE YOUR GO-TO

Have a ready list of favorite movies or songs that you can play when you need to change your mood or make a shift inside you. Consider making your alarm or ringtone a happy song that instantly fills you with joy (this turns something that you might normally dread, like getting up for work, into something joyful).

Avoid the Triggers that Can Get in Your Way

Triggers from the past can linger in your mind like the smell of rotting fish. They can impact every one of your relationships because when you deal with other people, you aren't just affected by your own triggers, you are affected by the other person's as well (because of how their triggers affect their *re.act.ions* and responses). If one of you chooses to heal, the other person's issues don't have as much power.

As you keep reading this chapter, I want you to keep this picture in mind. The circles in the image equate to time periods in your life. If you look at the image, imagine the left side is the past, the center is the present, and the right is the future. They are all interconnected (one circle) and each realm impacts the other.

When you heal the pain in your past, whether it is in that first layer (the immediate past) or the circle farthest out (childhood pain), it changes the cellular perception inside you on all levels: hormonal, immune, neurological, etc. These in turn affect the layers of your future and the reality of your present.

Look at the shades of color on each circle and think of them as representative of the evolution of your consciousness. Healing your past pain heals you on different levels of all realms of the circle of life. The impact ripples through you, giving you depth, realization, forgiveness, and a new perception of reality. *Re.member*, when you overcome your traumas, you stop making the same mistakes, and you start leveling up in the Game of Life.

You don't have to go in order with the circles. Feel free to jump around, pick a different area each time. Maybe post this image on your mirror and look at it each day as you decide what you want to work on within yourself.

A friend of mine recently went to a family reunion that was long overdue after years of strife in the family. The family took a group photo, and my friend, overjoyed by this family get together, shared the photo on social media. That post ended up creating a family war that my friend never conceived would happen. She had posted the image with good *intent.ions*, not realizing that the photo would cause other people's past issues to come to the surface, resulting in a lot of hurtful words.

My friend was stunned. I reminded her that even though you may visualize something one way, other people have their own triggers (often unbeknownst to you) which can change the outcome. The only way to keep these things from spiraling into more negativity is to control how you respond and how you choose to let the moment affect you. Think of it this way—if everyone on a ship starts to panic during a storm, they could capsize the boat. But if the captain stays calm and focuses on keeping the ship on the right path, everyone gets to the destination safely. You can't control the other people, but you can be a good captain to yourself.

Time Travel & Playing the Blame Game

There are two other potholes that you can run into that create an endless loop of hurt and negativity. The first, which I call "Time Travel," happens when a past memory that was never healed or forgiven keeps resurfacing in the present time. Like when you are having an argument with your loved one and they mention the time you lied about something many years ago. The same arguments and issues get recycled over and over again because whatever is happening in the moment is bringing those to light for the other person.

What can you do in that moment? Let it go.

Unfortunately, as we talked about earlier, you can only heal yourself, not others. That's on them. Hopefully, your inner work will rub off onto them because of the loving vibe you are sending from your heart. If it doesn't, then go back to your song or movie that makes you feel positive and upbeat, and vibe your imagination to that beat.

The "Blame Game" is when you choose to blame other people for the circumstances in your own life. This not only creates negativity but it keeps you from perceiving that you are the one in control of your future—not other people.

When you heal (forgive) your past, that *act.ion* creates a wonderful circle of healing that builds a more wonderful future than you have imagined. For example, maybe you hate going to your in-laws' house for dinner on Sundays. Stop and ask yourself *why* these visits bother you so much. Then picture yourself putting on a shield of protection between you and other people's negativity. Imagine going to Sunday dinner feeling happy and with love in your heart. When you do this, you are not affected by what other people say or do because you are committed to being in a positive state of mind and *choose* to perceive them with compassion. Being this way increases your vibe and increases the amount of love in the world. The outcome at the in-laws' will be more positive because you are choosing to let comments bounce off you, thereby not affecting your mood.

Use the Power of Visualization

Visualization is the key to succeeding in using your imagination because it gives you a walk-through, essentially, before these difficult moments happen. When you visualize a meeting you would normally dread and perceive it as one that rejuvenates you, those thoughts have the power to shift all the energy in the room and change the outcome for every single person.

But what if all that doesn't work? Maybe you aren't accepting your own part in these traps. If you are continuing to have the same arguments or run into the same roadblocks over and over again even after you have imagined a different outcome, then maybe it's time to have an honest conversation with yourself.

Have you healed and forgiven or are you time traveling to the past and pulling up that old memory, which makes you keep *re.act.ing* with judgment, blame, resentment, hurt, and/or worthlessness?

Don't undermine your own best efforts with stubbornness. You can block your amazing future and dull the power of your imagination by refusing to forgive. It doesn't matter if you have ten thousand reasons to never forgive the other person; you have to learn how to do it because forgiveness is not for others; it is 100% for you. Forgiveness allows a blocked heart to flow again. It opens the way for *love* to flow through us and to us.

You won't change overnight, but you can change a little each day. Every time you catch yourself *re.act.ing* to a trigger or falling into a trap, *re.member* that you have a chance right now to choose differently. You have the choice to see the future you in every now moment and be that you now.

Healing your past hurt/trauma means getting to the heart of the matter and asking yourself why you are so hell-bent on holding on to something that doesn't serve your best interests.

My friend from the story above ended up calling her family and telling them that she was sorry for any hurt or harm she caused them and she loved them. If her family doesn't respond or change, that's on them, not my friend. She broke the patterns of the past by taking *act.ion* quickly, owning up to her choices, and ending the conversation on a loving note. You can only break your patterns—and the power they hold over you—by facing your mistakes and choices, not avoiding them or creating a fight. That is how you play the Game with your heart focused on positive outcomes.

With every choice you make, you are creating a legacy, just as my father did. What positive imprint on others will you be *re.membered* for? I see you and all the good you will do. The bigger question is: **Do YOU see you?**

THE TRUTH YOU SHOULD KNOW

You are accountable for you—how you *re.act*/respond and how you perceive life. If you are feeling like you are covered in negative thoughts or that the people around you have filled you with their negative toxicity, take a shower. Literally, take a shower and imagine all that yuck coming out of you and washing down the drain.

Doing this means making a conscious choice to let stuff go. That's how you play the Game of Life with intention and in rhythm with the world. Every choice you make, every word you say is creating a legacy like my dad did with his stories. Before you say that thing or take that *act.ion*, think about how you want to be *re.membered*—full of negativity or as a positive beacon for everyone around you?

YOUR DASH ACT.ION

Imagine your phone is a remote control. When you wake up, instead of flipping through emails and social media, point the phone at the wall and select your personal movie channel because you are the director of your own movie (life). Imagine your life movie in full 3-D (or 5-D) and in beautiful Technicolor. What colors are around you, what does the scenery look like, how do you dress? What people are around you? What music is playing—is it classical, pop, jazz, hip-hop? How do you contribute to the world by helping others in a positive way and shining your inner light?

How can you edit that movie and rewrite it to be more loving, joyful, exciting, passionate, forgiving, purposeful, spontaneous, and heart-centered? What kind of ending do you want for each scene and moment? Using a highly-detailed imagination can be very powerful and effective.

SOMETIMES ALL YOU NEED IS AN EDIT

Directors edit movies to take out the bad parts and make the good parts have more impact. Sometimes, the edits they choose to make come after all the scenes are done and the movie has shifted in tone and message. Did you realize that you can do the same?

If you've ever visited your elementary school as an adult, you see that all those bathrooms and desks that were once intimidating are now small and not scary at all. A lot of your past is like *Jaws,* outdated and not as scary or traumatic as you imagined in your mind.

You are growing and changing every day. Revisit some of those past events and see them differently, through the lens of someone who is playing the Game of Life with intention and positivity. Realize that the people that hurt us were hurt, too. Hurt people *hurt* people. Forgive and move on.

Imagine that past pain as a blob of mud on your soul, mind, and body. Visualize it running off you and washing down the drain.

Or you can do the same thing with breathwork in a meditation session or writing in your journal. Use whatever resonates with you. Editing is a pathway to accomplish that magnificent future you desire.

TAKE INTENTIONAL ACTIONS

On Level 1, we discussed *e.motions* and their impact on how we see the world. On Level 2, we talked about our thoughts, how they affect us, how they lead to our *e.motions* (energy in motion), and end with *act.ion*. Those three things are connected like the example of the guitar.

On Level 3, we will learn how to "fine-tune" the string so our *e.motions* will create the visualization of the outcome we desire and show us the *intent.ional act.ions* we need to take to get there.

CHAPTER 7

DON'T SWEAT THE DETOURS AND SETBACKS

"Everything is energy. Match the frequency of the reality you want and you cannot help but get that reality. It can be no other way. This is not philosophy. This is physics."

ALBERT EINSTEIN

Have you ever seen or played Candy Land? If you have, then you've surely encountered the Peppermint Stick Forest, Peanut Brittle House, Molasses Swamp, and the Gumdrop Mountain. It's a simple game designed to inspire imagination in children. It also happens to be a pretty good reflection of how the Game of Life works because the path to winning, in both Candy Land and life, is always filled with detours and roadblocks.

In a board game, chances are you only have a single path to follow but in the Game of Life we are taking several roads at once—personal, family, spiritual, professional, physical, and financial. These roads can spring up in a variety of environments and all have different potential setbacks. However, if you trust from the start that these roads will be an adventure, the destination will be that much easier and more enjoyable to reach.

Ride the Lazy River Your Way

A few years ago, I took my kids to a waterpark in Florida that had this amazing lazy river. Along the route there were several waterfalls, beautiful tropical features, sections that added speed, others that slowed you down, and the inevitable traffic jams in narrow sections. The first go-round I wanted to do everything in my power to avoid the waterfalls (no one likes to be purposely doused with water), but my kids teamed up to ensure sure I couldn't avoid it. Every time we neared a waterfall, they pushed me into the middle, right under the heaviest part. I got drenched. I could have gotten angry (and saw many parents who did), but when I saw my kids laughing and enjoying the moment, I laughed, too.

At that juncture with the waterfall, I had a choice. Accept my fate and make the best of it by laughing with them or start yelling and storm off. We were in the water, however, and getting wet was part of the journey.

As we neared the second waterfall, I saw another mother and her kids just ahead of us. She ended up being bumped into the center of the water and when she got soaked, she let everyone around her know how angry she was. My kids asked me why someone would get that mad about getting wet at a waterpark. I told them that sometimes people get mad when life doesn't happen exactly the way they want it to and some people are just unhappy inside and it shows up in their *act.ions*.

The Captain Obvious answer is that risks are part of the experience and we should all just flow with whatever happens. Maybe there's a lesson for them to learn or that experience is preparing them for something even bigger and better. It's not always clear in the moment what the purpose of that experience is, and for many people, the waterfalls, potholes, and detours are infuriating instead of educating.

The Purpose of Potholes in Life

We all take risks and hit setbacks and rarely, if ever, know how they will turn out. When you gamble, you risk losing money or winning the jackpot. When you date, you risk having your heart broken or finding your soulmate. When you share your struggles, you risk being hurt by people close to you or being supported. You can't avoid risk. It is simply part of life.

So, what do you do when you are approaching a waterfall (or one comes out of left field)? You can choose to see the upside. I didn't plan on getting drenched, but I knew there was a chance; I accepted that risk as part of the experience the second I got into the lazy river. As it turned out, seeing my kids laugh so hard when we went under that waterfall was one of the best parts of that day.

I had prepared myself mentally for the waterfall, and that made a big difference in how I responded. Because of that, it turned out to be one of my favorite memories. It is in taking risks (and learning from those lessons) that we expand our consciousness to get to the next level.

I'm hoping that angry mother didn't let that one moment ruin the rest of her day or her kids' day. We all get angry, irritated, or frustrated. That's totally normal. However, it's not worth holding on to things that happen because then we end up making a big deal out of nothing at all. When the water first crashed down on me, my instinct was to pull away and I felt a flash of annoyance. Just as quickly as that happened, however, I let those feelings go. I didn't *re.act* with instant emotion; I took a moment to let my prefrontal cortex respond, and as a result, we had a fabulous day.

If you've ever gone on a road trip, you've hit forks in the road. In the days before cell phones and GPS, you had to make a decision: right or left. If you chose incorrectly, you could end up lost or hours from your original destination. You get to choose how you respond to the detour—are you going to make the most of it and grab a burger at that cute roadside diner or are you going to curse and stew the rest of the day, making the trip miserable for yourself and everyone in the car with you?

There are other forks in the road that we hit in our journey. Do we choose this person or that one, this new job or stay with the old one, this town to live in or that one we've never visited before? These can be critical deciding moments that boil down to a simple question: *do you go with the flow (listen to your intuition) or try to control your direction (overthink it and force it for all the wrong reasons)?*

If you are wondering which of the two choices is better, ask yourself which one *feels* better inside. Notice the feeling you receive as you imagine both choices. Trust your intuition to direct you.

When people start imagining different options, some allow their anxiety to kick in (as if they're listening to that song, "Should I Stay or Should I Go?"), along with all kinds of other *e.motions*, rather than just letting their soul experience what is.

You will undoubtedly have a choice like that come up. Maybe you get a job offer for the same pay and have to choose between staying in a job you don't like or taking a risk on the unknown. Or maybe the contract on the house you wanted falls apart. Do you pick a new one or get upset trying to make it happen anyway? In those moments, you have the choice to make a difference in your life and, by extension, the lives of those around you. Is that experience going to be positive or negative? To know that answer, go within your heart, breathe, and listen to your inner guidance.

You are reading this book for a reason; therefore, I know you desire to be a positive influence for yourself and those around you. Thank you for being here and thank you for being you.

Learn to look at road bumps through a different lens. Sometimes that bumpy path that seems difficult and awful is actually a chance to expand your consciousness and grow more. When you stop going over the same bumps and begin to change your path because you have learned to perceive things differently, you experience that first shift of awareness. You realize you have learned that lesson already (been there, done that) and can now avoid that same pothole. Your mission in the Game is to help others recognize and learn to avoid their own potholes.

Imagine yourself in the middle of a fast-moving river. The current is super strong and instead of riding with it, you cling to the banks, afraid to let go. That current is either going to rip you apart or become blocked as pieces of wood collect in the space around you (which is the collective consciousness of a group of people who *be.LIE.ve* something strongly and hold tight to a false narrative). Eventually, the river gets so clogged up it floods the land (and harms innocent people).

Let go and let it flow. Let the vibrations flow through you. Think of how freeing it would feel to let go of the riverbank and simply enjoy the ride! This relates to all paths in life: financial, relationship, professional, spiritual. Whatever you are holding on to for dear life is blocking you from moving forward. Release your grip.

> When you hit a detour or a bump in the road (like a Go to Jail card in Monopoly), *re.member* that this is an opportunity to perceive life differently and choose a joyful attitude. Play the Game by being mindfully aware of things you are holding on to too tightly and the mental cords binding you to old ways that hold you back. Cut those cords.

What Does the Flat Tire Mean to You?

A year ago, I was on my way to a friend's house when I got a flat tire. It stopped me, quite literally, in the middle of the road, and left me with a choice to make in how I responded. What flat tires have you experienced? Maybe an event you were looking forward to was canceled, or you went on a few dates with someone, only to find out they weren't as into you as much as you were into them. Knowing how you respond right now to the flat tires and potholes in life, as opposed to how you *intend* to respond, can help you build the right *intent.ional act.ions* for a less frustrating future.

Which person are you?

1. **"The Flat Ruins Everything" Person**: The flat tire ruins your entire day. That one event sets into motion a series of like events that confirm the day is awful.

Maybe you are late for an important meeting, miss a deadline that afternoon, or have to work through lunch. People who fall into this category talk about the flat tire all day long, holding on to it for as long as they possible can, focusing on the negatives instead of the positives.

Re.member, you are a magnet. You attract what you put out. To remind yourself of the electromagnetic field you choose to attract, stick a magnet on your desk or by the sink, anywhere that will be a constant reminder to change the energy you are putting out in order to change the energy you get back.

2. **"The Flat is a Temporary Inconvenience" Person**: The flat tire is just a temporary problem. You call AAA or change the tire yourself and then—and this is important—go about your day, leaving that small detour in the past. Your attitude about the flat might be something like: *I'm grateful that flat happened because I'm sure there was a reason why I got the flat tire. Maybe it saved me from being in an accident. Or maybe it was just a reminder for me to slow down and breathe.* The Temporary Inconvenience Person embraces the situation and trusts that it was meant to be, even if they can't see why right now.

When you choose to flow with a situation, you think, feel, and act with a high vibe. That response opens the door to perceiving life differently.

The Time Limit Trick

Games have timers that either measure when the Game will end or how long a player has to make a move. Since life is a Game, too, you can use a timer to your advantage when you hit a roadblock or detour.

When I was a teenager and going through my first real breakup, I cried endlessly. My dad came in my room and sat next to me on the bed. "This is good," he said. "Feel it, let it out, cry all you want. You have forty-eight hours."

I actually stopped crying. "Wait, what? Why forty-eight hours?"

I didn't realize it then, but he was shifting my focus by giving me numbers to think about (which creates a left brain/right brain shift, as I mentioned earlier). He told me that I should allow myself twenty-four hours to feel the heartache, then at halftime in my forty-eight hours, I should begin thinking about the positive side of this breakup. A football team talks strategy at halftime, he explained, and I should be doing the same by looking at my life ahead without this person.

Now I had a timetable to meet and that helped take my attention away from all that crying. My father reminded me that I shouldn't waste my life on something that had already happened because I can't go back and change it. I should allow myself to feel the pain, embrace it, and then begin healing. I asked him how on earth I could do that when my heart was so broken.

My dad asked me what things about my boyfriend had bothered me while I was dating him.

"Nothing," I said. "He was perfect."

My dad laughed. "You don't like the way he drives, he's always late, he flirts with other girls in front of you. What else bugged you about him?"

He had a valid point. The boyfriend wasn't as perfect as I thought, which meant there might also be positive aspects of this breakup that I hadn't thought about before. I took my dad's advice and used the next twenty-four hours to plan a strategy for healing. After that time passed, I began going out with my friends, working through my *e.motions*, and refusing to dwell in that sadness any longer. A week later, the guy who had broken up with me asked if we could get back together. I told him no. I had moved on and, in the process, realized he wasn't the one for me. In the end, we became friends but we never dated again.

I want to be clear here that my dad wasn't saying that you only need two days to heal your grief and heartache. His point was not to get too caught up in that heartache and lose myself.

Other sad events have happened in my life, and there have been times when I told myself I am choosing to feel the grief a lot longer. The key was that I chose that feeling, instead of letting those feelings control me. That's an important shift to make.

The void of a loss may last a lifetime; it's the depth of your grief and sorrow that you need to be mindfully aware about. When you choose not to be consumed by your grief, you are lessening the intensity of that emotion while also embracing your own willingness to move out of the low vibe it creates. We are here to experience and face challenges, and either live in sorrow or shift to courage in order to move forward. *Re.member*, opting for the higher vibe brings love and peace to you.

Grief is a process, so you should honor the love you shared and also know that love never dies, it simply transforms. I realize that is not the same as having that loved one here on earth. I lost my dad and brother more than three decades ago and from time to time, I still have *e.motions* that rise to the surface. I acknowledge the feelings, embrace them, and allow the grief to run through me.

I don't want to downplay the feelings of grief and the necessity of going through the stages. Take whatever time you need because everyone is different and every person's process is different. If you feel like you can't move forward, it's important to seek help and give yourself grace.

Setting Intent.ional Responses for the Future

You're going to hit a roadblock or detour in the future; that's inevitable. When you do, you have a choice about how you are going to respond. By practicing and learning your *intent. ional* responses ahead of time, you begin carving out new neural pathways and a different future. Here are two quick exercises to practice this:

Exercise One

Think of a time in your life when you controlled everything about a particular situation, to the point where you were stressed out, anxious, and overwhelmed.

Now, visualize that same moment differently in your mind (as if you are watching a movie). See yourself taking a step back, giving yourself time to let it go or responding in a more positive manner and ask yourself these questions:

- *How would the situation have turned out differently?*

- *What is the worst thing that would have happened if you responded in this way?*

- *Would it be as awful as you think? Or would it have an even better outcome than you imagined?*

- *Would letting go, even a little, have changed anything?*

- *If you end up in that same situation, what would you do differently? How would the new you respond and act?*

For example, one of my friends moved recently and when I called her, she was completely consumed with the packing and the details. She wouldn't go to lunch, go out with her friends, or take a break. She told me she couldn't sleep because she was so stressed out. Yes, moving is stressful, sometimes *very* stressful, but taking a step back and having fun with the people you may never see again is important for your physical body, soul, and mind.

> We have more control than we realize when we go with the flow. Be open to whatever comes your way because then you are also open to receiving, which means the Universe will manifest your *intent.ions* in time.

I asked her what would be the worst possible outcome if she took that night off to see her friends. She was afraid the packing wouldn't get finished or the boxes wouldn't be labeled correctly. She was consumed by the need to control every box that was packed. In reality, anyone can write a summary of items on a box and label it with a room. She could hire movers or ask her friends to help. Both options would reduce her stress.

I have made five major moves in three years. I know the stress of packing and the *e.motions* that come with it. With the power of hindsight, I wish I had been less stressed, or at the very least, allowed myself to feel the *e.motions* instead of packing them up in a box with the pots and pans. That box gets unpacked sooner or later; the choice is yours.

Exercise Two

Now, think of a time in your life when you felt helpless and had no control (like being on the lazy river and heading straight for the waterfall). Maybe you're thinking *poor little me, nothing good ever happens for me. Life just keeps throwing me lemons.* When you set that kind of vibe into motion, you are creating a negative mindset, so expect to perceive everything as negative.

Maybe life did throw you a bunch of lemons. Ask yourself these questions:

- *What's the worst thing that could happen? The lemonade is too tart?*

- *Did you learn a lot of lessons that helped you level up in consciousness?*

- *If that does happen, will the outcome be as bad as you think?*

- *What positive outcomes could come of this?*

- *Is there something you can do to shift or change the situation to see it differently ("let me see that differently")?*

I know two people who lost a job. This was an event that was not in their control. There was nothing they could do to change that situation—*except how they chose to handle it.* Both were stressed, both worried about money, and both felt devastated. I get it. Losing your job is a very stressful event. This is a major detour and taking the time to catch your breath is necessary.

One friend abided by the forty-eight-hour rule. She had a pity party for one day, took the next day to enjoy some time in the sun with friends, then started looking for work. The other friend let the sadness, anxiety, and stress from losing her job consume her. For weeks, she stayed stuck in her sadness and grief. She sat on the couch, binged *tell.A.vision*, and lost all motivation to look for work.

Guess which of my friends got a job within a week? And a better job than before, at that?

When you get sent to jail in Monopoly, it gives you a chance to look at the whole board. You can see where your opponent's properties are, how much money they have to play with, and what moves they are making. It gives you time to breathe and strategize. Maybe getting sent to jail kept you from landing on Park Place (and paying the steep rent to another player). Maybe it allowed you time to develop a new strategy, based on how your opponents are playing. Don't wallow in the anxiety and frustration of this detour. **Reframe** your situation and begin looking for the growth opportunities. Take a minute to imagine your ideal solution and then set a time frame to have it occur. Trust that it will happen.

When one door closes, other doors open, so always be mindful and ask the Universe to see those other doors. When I do that, I say, "Make it obvious and repeat it three times so I know it's a sign."

A Note About U-turns

A U-turn is a complete change of direction. A U-turn gives you the opportunity to see the other side of the road, like the front side of our body is different than the back side. This is a SHIFT in a major way. Think about your life from all angles: professionally, socially, financially, spiritually, physically. What would happen if you flipped those images of yourself upside down? For instance, maybe you hate to exercise. How would you see yourself if you became someone who went to the gym regularly? Maybe you wish you spoke up more at work? How would the you who is vocal behave in a meeting? What if you stopped eating junk food, or stopped drinking or gave up *tell. LIE.vison*, or started working out? What's stopping you from doing those things? They're just a simple U-turn. Yes, this U-turn of self might feel foreign at first, but eventually you will grow into this new you.

> "Begin observing your thoughts and notice if you're going in the wrong direction. You can, with conscious effort, make a U-turn with new thoughts."
>
> —Dr. Wayne Dryer

A U-turn can be as simple as going from being an employee to an entrepreneur; never exercising to exercising daily; drinking alcohol to not drinking at all; living paycheck to paycheck to no worries financially; no spiritual practice to a non-negotiable spiritual practice. Take a few minutes, explore each area of your life, and perceive the opposite. Entertain the idea of the other side of the road.

This is what happens inside you when you realize that you are dissolving and crumbling the walls of limitation that were put in place by society to keep you thinking small, feeling worthless, and living limited. Now, you can think of yourself as big, powerful, limitless. Once you apply the principles of raising your vibration, the U-turn doesn't take that long and you're on that road to an abundant life that much sooner.

Share your high vibration with those around you so that your electromagnetic field of energy creates a wave that it is **a very powerful force**. Think of it rippling out to the people around you, and all of those people combining to become a force of great change. There will be those who choose to stay in a lower frequency—that is their pathway and their journey. Honor them by sending much love to them. Your journey is in moving forward with others who want to bring about a shift in the world.

> Everything you do or don't do matters, that is how powerful you are, that is the true power hidden within. Let the walls of your *be.LIE.f* crumble, shake them off and set yourself free.

In the Bible, the Wall of Jericho (Joshua 6:20) came tumbling down because of the vibrational frequency of the people who spent seven days marching around the wall and singing. Their collective vibration literally tore down a stone wall. If a few people can do that, imagine what you can do when you choose to crumble the walls (*be.LIE.fs*) you are holding on to within you and how that will encourage others to do the same.

THE TRUTH YOU SHOULD KNOW

Potholes are part of life; they give us opportunities to learn, grow, evolve, and act differently next time one appears in our pathway. When you take an *act.ion*, you, and only you, are accountable and responsible for that *act.ion*, be it good or bad. **No one, absolutely no one else, is responsible for your *act.ions*.**

YOUR DASH ACT.ION

Today, when you hit a pothole, detour, or setback, I want you to imagine yourself driving around it. This is not avoidance because you are mindfully aware of the obstacle and are simply choosing to not experience it again. You have learned your lesson and are able to see the pothole before you fall into the hole. Now, imagine the brighter destination that waits on the other side. Hold on to that feeling of love and light and create a more positive vibe for the rest of your day.

TRIGGER WORDS

Trigger words can trip you up and send you backward in the Game of Life. It is up to you whether to be triggered or not, whether to let the words go or not. Words have many meanings and can be taken in many different ways.

For instance, the word "slave," which I used earlier in the book. I am not using that word to depict, insult, or in any way demean a race, gender, or religion. When I say "slave," I am not talking about the slaves that were forced to work and abused for decades. I am talking about the external things that enslave us. We are **all** 100% a slave to this society and we don't even know it.

We are enslaved to debt. To material things. To social media. To keeping up with the Joneses. These things control our every mood, thought, purchase, and moment.

I am asking you to cancel/clear and erase all labels, meaning all of the programming you have about certain words. The Game of Life is about freeing ourselves on every conceivable level and unleashing our true power. Together, we can and will break the chains of every aspect of society and become free. This concept is much bigger than what we are diving into in this book, so I encourage you to learn more about the **great awakening** that is happening.

Taking a U-turn (perceiving life from the opposite direction) and tearing down our inner walls help each of us go through a complete metamorphosis of mind, body, and spirit, both internally and externally, so that we can start seeing what is hidden in plain sight and learn the true power within our hearts.

We can do this together *and* individually. That, my friends, is the **premise** of the Game of Life.

CHAPTER 8

UPGRADE
YOUR GAME

"Optimism is a strategy for making a better future. Because
unless you believe that the future can be better, you are
unlikely to step up and take responsibility for making it so."

NOAM CHOMSKY

As you move through the Game of Life and begin to make
new, conscious decisions, you reach a higher dimension inside
yourself. You have a new perspective on life and inner-stand
with a deeper knowing the power of Natural Laws and God's
law. With this inner power you are gaining freedom and
empowerment on all levels of your mind, body, spirit, and soul.

Fear becomes a challenge to conquer so that you can then help others reach the same level.

Throughout the process, you are undergoing a metamorphosis, much like a caterpillar does when it becomes a butterfly. You are completely shedding your old self to emerge as a brighter, more beautiful soul. However, getting there requires a fair amount of courage and the willingness to let go of constructs that you have been holding on to like crutches for most of your life.

Your Butterfly Journey

We start our lives as infants, unable to do anything on our own and completely reliant on others for food, clothing, and shelter. Then we learn to crawl and walk, and start becoming curious about the world. We learn the stove is hot, the sky is blue, and that if we flip a switch, lights come on.

As we navigate the world through our childhood and teenage years, each new phase of our lives brings another insight. All this information and the experiences we have are constantly changing and impacting this new version of ourselves. But somewhere along the way when we become adults, we stop becoming a new version of ourselves. We get stuck in a mindset of repeating the same things over and over, and never challenging ourselves to think in a different direction or experience a new challenge. We say things like: "I'm too old to learn new things" or "My time to do that was years ago."

Do you know anyone whose main topic of conversation is what they recently watched on *tell.LIE.vision* or a streaming service?

Do they go to the same hangouts as they did twenty or thirty years ago? Their lives are a repeat, day after day, with patterns so regular you could set your watch by them. Or maybe this describes the rut you are stuck in, the place you have settled into, like a comfortable couch. Society has certainly made this acceptable mindset very comfy.

To me, this is like going to jail in a Game of Monopoly and never leaving so that you can get back to playing the game. Maybe you've grown content with just getting by and have become a slave to societal expectations and are feeling powerless.

It's easy to get stuck in that rut and requires a conscious choice to escape it.

There is an amazing reward for those who embrace change and work daily to become their best self—acceptance, love, appreciation, value, and inner peace. Once you set out on this journey, you learn that discovering your hidden true self, special abilities, and unique talents is fun, exciting, and most of all, **liberating**, like a new butterfly taking flight.

Before that butterfly can emerge into its new life, however, the caterpillar has to eat like crazy and grow quickly (during its learning phase) in order to prepare for this transformation (this is your self-discovery phase where you take an honest look at yourself, face your fears head-on, and choose to accept and forgive yourself and others).

As the caterpillar creates the cocoon, it literally dissolves its entire body into this gooey mess of cells (this is you shedding the friends, lifestyle, and influences that aren't serving your highest self). A couple weeks later, the cocoon breaks open and a truly remarkable, beautiful butterfly emerges (this is when you have become your highest self and can see all that was hidden from you in the world with new *eYe*s and a new perspective). Only then, after undergoing a difficult process, is the butterfly ready to take on the world and help create more butterflies.

When you are in the cocoon, you are busy discovering who you are, what you want to be and do, what strengths and weaknesses you have, and which are the virtuous and inferior parts of your existence. You begin to question your core *be.LIE.f* systems and embrace your curiosity, making you open to learning and *inner. standing*. Questioning everything you think you know is key to this growth.

For example: Let's say you grew up in a family that told you wearing yellow on Mondays is the only way to get into college and those who don't wear yellow won't get into college. This *be.LIE.f* is reinforced in what you learn in school, what you hear from others, and what you read and listen to. Everyone you know *be.LIE.ves* this to be true. No one knows why it's true; they just *be.LIE.ve* it wholeheartedly. If enough people are taught something (even if it's a lie), it becomes part of the *cult. ure* and is accepted as true by most.

But you dislike the color yellow and don't want to wear it on Mondays or any other day. You begin to question this *be.LIE.f* and start to research why yellow and why Mondays and why it affects college acceptance rates. You find out, by digging deeper, that in truth it doesn't matter what color you wear on Monday or any day; getting into college has nothing at all to do with colors or days of the week. This dissolves all your prior *be.LIE. fs* (the cocoon stage) and allows you the space to begin thinking in new ways.

When you emerge as a butterfly, you realize that just because someone says something is true, it isn't necessarily (like Santa). That open thinking allows your mind to explore new ways of being and allows you to begin building your best and most beautiful self.

> To become a butterfly, you need to accept the challenge to question all your core *be.LIE.fs* and ask yourself: Do I know these *be.LIE.fs* are true? If they aren't, is it okay? What does that mean for me and for the world if this *be.LIE.f* is not true?

Asking these questions can be earth-shattering for the mind. It rocks you to the core to find out something or someone you really *be.LIE.ved* was evil is good or something that was labeled as good is super evil. Maybe there's an event you were told was fake that turns out to be real or something we all thought was a real event (a major one) turns out to be a Hollywood production designed to create an *ill.u.sion* that society wanted us collectively to *be.LIE.ve*, in order to evoke a separation amongst us.

163

All this information might be overwhelming at first, but trust the process as you begin to crawl, then walk, and finally run. It can be exciting and fun and make you feel alive, desiring more and more knowledge. The butterfly version of you will soar to new heights and discover a new world inside the one you have been living in all this time.

> If you want to become the best version of yourself, pretend you are an actor playing that person. See, hear, feel the person you want to be. This can work with a simple habit change like biting your nails. See yourself with long nails, feel them, desire them, and then you can recognize the habit and change it.

The Metamorphosis of Mindfulness

The metamorphosis phase involves some serious inner work (mentally, spiritually, and physically), but once you get through the first few hard-core earth-shattering realizations, it becomes easier. The cells in your body begin to feel the shift and it becomes more natural. No matter what the transformation brings, you know you will be okay with whatever happens because at the end of the day, the world goes on and the sun will rise.

These cellular level changes mean you might start eating differently or have different desires, interests, and friends. There can be periods of isolation because you want to be alone. I was always very social but as I did more inner work, I got to the point where I didn't want to go out at all unless it was for a walk in nature. From time to time, I would regress and fall back into my old bad habits of eating sugar, going out, etc. When I did that, however, I found I didn't relate to people the same way as I had before, my favorite dessert didn't taste as good, and I wasn't as happy in that old world. I liken this to going back to your grade school and realizing how small the desks are (when they seemed so big years before) because you have outgrown the old you.

> The miracles of life that are hidden surround us at all times are just waiting to be found once we go within.

Becoming the butterfly is our soul's mission for being here. We are here to explore, evolve, transform to higher consciousness, and to see life from an observer's view. When you do that, you realize you control more in the Game of Life than you ever thought possible.

Re.member the guitar analogy? As you learn to control/fine-tune your thoughts and *e.motions*, you become mindfully aware of your *act.ions*. Your mind, body, and soul's ability to shift perspectives at will increases. You are more *aware,* on every level, and it's an amazing feeling.

Being mindful is a continual process. Everybody slips back into old habits from time to time. If you notice you are starting to take things personally, or you are feeling sad, anxious, afraid, powerless, unworthy, trapped, and other low vibrations, then it's time to **stop**. That is **not you anymore.**

That's why the Dash Act.ions included at the end of each chapter are so important. If you do them without any real intention behind your *act.ions*, that's like thinking about running instead of actually physically running. You won't get in shape that way, just as you won't get in mental shape by not taking the Dash Act.ions seriously.

Feel these Dash Act.ions at a cellular level in your body. Go deep within and truly experience the *e.motions* you will feel when you reach those desired outcomes. That will help you to better focus your *intent.ions*, which in turn allows you to take *act.ion* with imagination, determination, confidence, power, and an inner calmness of knowing and trusting the process.

None of this happens overnight. Just as you can't buy running shoes on Monday and run ten miles on Tuesday, you need to build up your mental muscles. As you push yourself a little more each day, your systems get used to a new rhythm, a new pattern. That's all really fabulous for you. You're building different routines and allowing your internal systems to get in line with your goals at a pace they can manage. On the flip side, if you aren't acting with intention or creating the daily habits around these changes you want to manifest, your results might happen, but not as quickly or as completely as you desire.

All of this is preparing you to create that internal shift that allows you to **respond rather than *re.act***. Do the exercise below to learn to create space between your *re.act.ions* and your responses.

The Building Resilience Exercise

Choose someone you know well.

Step One: Gratitude and Trust

a. You and a friend write down the different ways you are grateful for each other.

b. Read what you wrote to each other.

c. After that, ask each other: *How do you feel?* I bet you're smiling and feeling good.

d. Thank one another for sharing.

Step Two: Listening and Sharing

(one will be a Sharer, the other a Listener, then switch).

a. Visualize a shield of protection around you, like a cocoon.

   i. What color and shape is it? Create a fun shield, one you can *re.member*. Picture it in your mind or draw it on a piece of paper. When someone with a low vibe comes into your bubble, imagine your shield protecting you. Perceive the anger or whatever low energy is coming at you as arrows bouncing off the shield and falling to the ground. Trust that you are protected.

   ii. Keep in mind all those kind, loving words you just heard about yourself, as well as your happy song or movie from the previous chapter.

        iii. Breathe mindfully to align your internal system, preparing the cells in your body to change.

   b. For the Sharer: think of a time in your life when someone hurt you or when you hurt someone with words or *act.ions*. What was said or done? Feel that memory, embrace this feeling.

        i. Start sharing that painful experience with the Listener. Maximum amount of share time: one to two minutes.

        ii. Don't feel the need to supplement the story with history. Those other events are all a broken record that no one wants to hear again.

        iii. Ask yourself: *Am I ready to change this situation?* If not, that's fine. You can choose to relive the moment until you are ready to let it go and learn the lesson.

        iv. Share only the facts, in a short and brief manner, as if you were the observer of the experience. You're summarizing, not drawing it out or justifying why you felt this way or that way. The sharing is for one or two minutes only.

   c. For the Listener: Listen with compassion and acceptance. Hear what is being said by the other person, without any judgement, blame, fault. This should be a safe zone for them.

      i. In one minute or less, repeat the essence of what you just heard. No solutions, nor advice. Just what you heard.

     ii. For the Sharer: Realize if you need to reword or adjust the experience. Sometimes when we hear someone repeat what they think they heard us say, we hear it differently, or a revelation might come to mind, or we realize we didn't explain it correctly.

    iii. The Listener should make sure the Sharer feels heard and valued.

  d. Switch roles and repeat the exercise

  e. When you are done, ask each other: *How do you feel?* Now thank each other.

By allowing someone else to observe an event in your life and then doing the same for another person, it teaches you to have an impartial bird's-*eYe* view of a future similar situation. You take the emotion out of the equation by being the Observer. This way you aren't caught off guard when someone triggers you with their words or *act.ions*. Take a step back and see what is happening as the Observer. Every time you do that, you're building your resilience.

You never know what other people are going through, and you can't control how they act because of that. You are responsible for yourself and how you treat others. When you set a higher, more intent.ional and positive vibe, it ripples outward like waves in a pond, impacting those around you.

Think about it: does the butterfly see another caterpillar and *re.member* how traumatic it was to go through the metamorphosis? Or does it fly above and enjoy life? The butterfly has a different perspective now and that gives it **true power**.

A couple of tips for when you do this exercise with a friend, or in the future, when a situation arises:

> **Don't take it personally**. Tell yourself you are NOT THAT PERSON ANYMORE. We all have moments when someone else's bad, low vibes come into our life whether that be anger, blame, fear, doom and gloom, sickness, or anxiety. *Re.member* your shield of protection and draw on that strength so that the arrow of their negative energy bounces off of you.

> **Become the Observer.** When someone does or says something that makes you upset, think about how you would explain it to someone else if you were just talking about the bare-bones facts. Does this still seem mean or

upsetting? Maybe you read more into it than was meant. Maybe the other person has things going on in their life that made them lash out or be less friendly (hurt people *hurt* people). Step back for a moment and look at all sides of the situation differently.

If what was said was *intent.ionally* mean, do you think the sender/speaker is someone who was hurt by something else? No matter what, let it go, breathe, use your shield of protection, and don't take it personally.

Feed your mind with intention through the words you choose.

Here's a simple example of becoming the Observer: A friend of mine works in contracts for a large company where the documents she creates go through negotiations. This requires both parties to go through and make changes called "redlines." My friend would interpret these redlines as offensive and get upset, as if a total stranger was trying to be mean by marking up a contract. I talked to her about being more *intent.ional* with her own redlines. She started adding nice words to explain the reason for the deletion, change, or addition. When she did this, redlining became a Game for her and she set an intention for a lovely correspondence of redline etiquette to take place. She controlled her response by taking the time to observe her communications. When she became more *intent.ional* and kinder in her redline notes, this created a positive vibration for the receiver, who was then better able to understand her position and respond in a similar manner (because the positivity has a ripple effect). Her negotiations became more pleasant, friendly, and successful.

Did it work 100% of the time? For the most part, yes, it did. There are always a few people who were in a bad mood no matter what and that was fine too, because she knew to not take it personally. When she had a difficult call to make, she paused to mentally cover herself with a shield of protection before she responded in a kind and calm way.

THE TRUTH YOU SHOULD KNOW

I'm sure you already know that your thoughts, *e.motions*, and *act.ions* are affected by what you "feed" them. If you are around negative people, watching mindless shows or constant news channels on *tell.LIE.vision*, it's akin to a runner eating fried food and drinking alcohol before a marathon. The run probably won't be successful, and the runner might not even finish. You have to feed your mind positively if you want to emerge a more positive, grounded person.

Don't get too comfortable in the traps of life because then you are literally living in the past or accepting a mediocre life and *thinking* you are present when you really aren't. Spend a week taking note of everything you read and watch, as well as the people you talk to and how their words make you feel.

Mindfully make different choices that leave you with a more positive vibe at the end of the day.

Stop feeding your mind junk food if you want to become the best version of you.

YOUR DASH ACT.ION

Do Toning techniques to get your thoughts and body aligned. Breathing and Toning are techniques we can use to bring about the change we desire in ourselves. We already talked about breathing. Toning is about focusing attention on and being aware of your breath.

Take a deep breath. As you breathe out, make a sound, any sound. This sound becomes your body's cue to harmonize and balance your systems. Do this several times until you feel like your energy is rising and your mind is clear. You can find several videos and a lot of information on Toning with a simple internet search. Take the *act.ion* step to look it up and then practice it regularly.

THE SCHUMANN
RESONANCE

Mother Earth has a natural heartbeat, which has a natural rhythm with frequency of 7.83 Hz. All living things are connected to this heartbeat, a phenomenon that can be measured with an electromagnetic spectrum known as the Schumann Resonance.

The frequency is an alpha/theta frequency like that in the human brain; it's the state of brainwave frequency of a relaxed, dreamy, sleepy state. Our entire biological system, the brain, and the earth itself work on the same frequencies. I find this fascinating because this ties back to the Natural Laws discussed in Chapter 1.

CHAPTER 9

MASTERING
THE END GAME

"Things change whether you want them to or not, unless you are dead. Don't hold so hard to the past that you die with it."

PATRICIA BRIGGS

In college I took a class on Death and Dying. That class gave me a different perspective on living life, not just surviving life and then dying. In class, we were shown clips of interviews with people who had faced death or near-death experiences. Their experiences and observations led me to question my own personal thoughts and *e.motions* about death.

Shortly after I graduated, several of my loved ones died around the same time. These deaths took me further down that pathway of self-discovery in questioning the meaning of life. The class had sparked my interest, but now I wanted to go deeper, so I read many books in search of more *inner.standing*.

When we lose a loved one, death can play mind tricks on us because the experience is so overwhelming and difficult to wrap our minds around. Losing someone who means a lot to you triggers a flood of *e.motions* and *re.act.ions*. The deeper the personal relationship with the person, the deeper the *e.motions* we experience. The bereavement process we go through will be unique to each of us and is affected by the *be.LIE.fs* we have about religion, death, faith, and spirituality.

Every single one of us is going to die someday. That's an unchangeable fact. Yet we fear dying and seldom discuss the topic of our own death with others or think about it ourselves. Why is that? Besides being born, death is the most significant thing that will happen to us, so it bears discussion and thought.

If you didn't fear dying, would you live differently? Would you be bolder, have more courage, take more risks, overcome sickness faster, laugh more? Is death the end game or the beginning of a new game? Pause and think about these questions.

We all work through our grief in a different way as we learn to live without the other person's physical presence. I once thought letting go meant losing my connection to them, but that is not true. **Letting go is about releasing the *e.motions* that are blocking us from living and being our best selves.** The sooner we can learn to embrace loss, the faster we can begin to perceive death with a new perspective and get back to living the way we were meant to live. As we talked about before, that doesn't mean you are healed and done with grieving. There are many layers to an onion and death has a multitude of layers for us to process.

If you are having trouble letting go, know that it's totally okay to cry. You just don't want to dwell in sadness for too long because you can slip into a darkness that can be difficult to climb out of again. There are several movies showing darkness taking over the world or a person, then a spark of light (love) inside the hero of the story saves the world (person), and the darkness retreats. That darkness is the deepest part of grief. It's okay to feel that loss (darkness) for a while and mourn the death of that relationship, but don't stay in that place for too long or you might lose yourself.

When you're ready and have worked through all the stages of your grief, take a deep breath and breathe in your life-force. *Re.member*, that person's love is still alive in your heart, always. Shift your mindset and find the spark inside you by keeping that loved one **alive in your heart with memories**. Honor those memories by looking for the positives you have gained after having loved and known them.

Choosing to find the good and positive, even in your grief, is important because it creates a light that will shine and be there whenever you start feeling the darkness of life creep in on you. Take a moment, breathe, and focus on one of your happy memories with that person. Those memories are a gift to be cherished because they are stored in our hearts and cells forever. By choosing to focus on the good, you become an example of moving forward to others.

Re.member, energy is neither created nor destroyed; it simply transforms from one form to another. At death our spark (our energy) is shared with our loved ones to be forever kept alive by the love in our hearts, the highest vibration possible. This is the Law of Perpetual Transmutation of Energy.

Everyone that passes away leaves an imprint on those left behind. This means that **everyone's life, including yours, does matter**. There is always someone changed, touched, affected by each one of us and thus, the love is held in the heart when they *re.member* us. What memories are you leaving behind, what difference are you making in the lives of those you love? Not just your family, but your friends, neighbors, even your coworkers. All of these people can and will be touched by your *act.ions* in some way. That's why now is the time to become your best self.

The Final Four

There are four golden tickets to leaving this world a better place than you found it. These "Final Four," as I call them, are crucial for every one of us to do because it truly is the path to creating a legacy of love.

1. **Repent**: We are accountable and responsible for all our *act.ions*, all the time. If you don't repent, you repeat. You will repeat the lesson over and over again until you learn from it, repent for your mistakes, and then release that experience. Life will test you by putting you in similar situations to give you an opportunity to choose differently. By not repenting (not choosing) to act differently, you stay stuck. You may experience the same lesson but with greater intensity because the Universe is trying to grab your attention so that you can recognize your sins/errors and ask for forgiveness. *"Forgive me my trespasses."*

2. **Forgiveness**: Forgiveness is the key to unblocking/ unlocking your trauma and allowing your life-force (water) to flow with the rhythm of life. To be successful at the Game of Life, you must release all your anger, resentment, hate, sadness, fear, jealousy, blame because holding on to these low vibrations can destroy you and prevent you from being your highest, best, and most divine self. You owe it to yourself and others to be your best self for the greater good of consciousness that connects us all. *Re.member* the circle of eternal life,

and ask yourself: *What if by not forgiving, I become (or come back as) that person I refused to forgive? Is that a risk I'm willing to take? Re.member: "As I forgive those that trespass against me."*

3. **Be of Service/Give Love**: To be of service to others is a HUGE reward, much greater than any monetary reward. Money comes and goes, and all of its value lies in acquiring material luxuries that you can't take with you when you die. Your love and service to others is a reward that is repaid tenfold on a spiritual level. Love is giving of yourself, showing kindness and compassion to others, and helping to make someone's life better.

4. **Gratitude**: Giving thanks for all you have helps increase your vibe as well as shift how you perceive life. When you give thanks for even the smallest things, you are telling your mind that this thing you are grateful for is good. Your mind will then set into motion the vibration that will give you more of the same. If you want more love, be thankful for all the love you have. If you want more beauty, be thankful for the face you see in the mirror. If you want more kindness, be thankful to all the kindness you are given. If you want to be healthier, give thanks daily for the health you do have.

The Final Four create an impact on your soul and leaves a legacy that is *re.membered*, not only in the minds of others, but also in their cells. Whether you *be.LIE.ve* in past lives or not, know that life is eternal. What you do in the here and now has a lifelong, lasting effect on eternity.

What if by mastering the Final Four you unravel your past errors and in doing so, create a better future for all your lineage (your children, siblings, parents, etc.). Would you think, feel, act differently today?

The End Game Exercise

At the end of your dash is your death date, and within that, your funeral and eulogy (which I call your life tribute). Before you do this exercise, take a moment to think about funerals you have been to and what was said about the person who died. Have you ever wondered or even considered what people will say about you at your funeral? Whether you want a somber occasion or a celebration of life after you are gone, don't just talk about it—plan it by taking those *act.ions* today.

My dad loved to take pictures of everyone and every event, then print the pictures and make a collage on our family room wall. Friends and neighbors would come over to find their picture on the Acker family wall. This brought so much joy to everyone and was truly a family room of love. When my dad passed away, my family and I printed dozens of photos and then took a large piece of cardboard and used those photos to make a huge collage of pictures of family and friends with him. As we made our way through the pile of pictures we told stories, shared a few secrets, and most of all, we laughed and cried. It was probably the best therapy our family could have had.

We brought the giant collage to the funeral home. Each person who looked at it had a story to share, making every single picture come alive. It was a treasure that I cherish to this day (and have hanging on the wall in my house). I swear my dad planned it all with those years and years of photos he accumulated. I'm sure his life tribute was exactly what he would have wanted.

Stop for a moment and reflect on your life. Then get out a piece of paper and write your life tribute that would be read at your funeral. Tell the world and your loved ones all of your true feelings about life, love, and happiness, as well as the challenges and victories you have achieved. Talk about what life meant to you and how each of them helped you become your best self. You can write down what you learned from being mad at them, losing them, loving them, and the adventures, enjoyment and journeys that shaped you.

Go within your heart and let it guide you in this exercise. Is there anything you need to say to anyone before you go? Have you told everyone that you love them? Have you faced your fears, lived your life to the fullest, taken risks, and embraced the lessons you learned? Is there something that you wanted to do but have put off? Write it down as if you have accomplished it already.

When you are finished writing this, think about who will read your tribute and how you envision your funeral. This is, after all, a tribute to you, so **plan the way you want to be** *re.membered*.

STOP PUTTING OFF LIVING

Do not fear death because your power is in the now. How and what you do today is in your control. Live your life as if today were your last day. And never, ever hold back from saying, "I love you, I'm sorry, please forgive me, thank you."

As I said earlier, energy is never created nor destroyed, it simply transforms. Take water for example. You can drink water and it becomes part of your body, or you can change it to steam or freeze it to make ice. The energy is transformed in different ways. Your energy will also transform when you die and this life tribute exercise is to help you visualize what you want that energy to convert into.

Update your life tribute periodically, maybe on January 1st or your birthday. When you do, reflect on what you did that year, what areas you can improve upon, what fears you faced, and what risks you took. What new exciting things did you add to your dash? Did you live your life the way you wanted to?

If you have questions about these topics, go to my website, www.TheGameofLife101.com for references, or you can research those things that intrigue you. You can also explore death meditations and books about near-death experiences that show dying with a different perspective.

Create A Powerful Circle of Life

The circle, which we used on this book's cover, represents the continuation of our ancestry. We have our birth, then our death, then the birth of the next generation. It is all a transmutation of energy. When a leaf falls off a tree, it decomposes (transfers its energy) into the soil to give nourishment, which goes to the roots of the tree, helping the tree grow and produce more leaves, and on and on. When we die, whatever vibe we have left behind goes to a loved one, transcending love through time and space. It becomes the nourishment for that person, if you have left behind a positive vibe.

Living life to the fullest is not just a catchy phrase, it's a requirement. The End Game is defined by our act. ions or lack thereof. Aim high but don't overlook the person in the mirror. You are precious and valuable, more than you realize. Be a hero in this Game, but always re.member to also give yourself self-care, self-love, and grace.

Re.member the first Universal Law? We are all one, which means what you do impacts everyone else. How you choose to live your life affects so much more than just you. If we all chose to live in a positive vibe, imagine the power that would have on the circle of life.

One drop of water in the ocean that is charged with passion (electromagnetic energy/electricity) will make a difference by causing a spark, that spark ignites other drops, and together they will create a wave, and when they work in rhythm, they can become a tidal wave. Together we can create a vibrational tidal wave of love, kindness, compassion, and acceptance that changes the course of history for the betterment of all living things.

It only takes a small percentage of us uniting together with a deliberate purpose to create a vibrational shift on this planet. Imagine what you can do now to become a part of that tidal wave, leaving a legacy that will be *re.membered* in history books. Each of us are pioneers of our now and can create, imagine, and live a now that changes the world of tomorrow.

Make your End Game legendary, with lasting memories that leave a monumental impact. That can be anything that makes life better—inventing revolutionary tools, helping a neighbor, creating a loving family, or simply creating fun events for your community. Whatever that is, always live each day as if it were your last.

Reboot Your Quantum Computer

Throughout this book we have talked about becoming your new, best self. You are essentially upgrading yourself, as you would a computer. When a computer gets an upgrade, the old version eventually becomes outdated and stops working. We all know someone who refuses to get a new computer and stop using Windows XP. The computer company stops offering support for that version and designers stop creating software that will work with it, so the computer is no longer operating at its peak efficiency. That's you, if you choose not to upgrade.

The old version is found in those people who remain inflexibly in a low vibration. These are the people who live in fear, jealousy, blame, judgement, resentment, hate, sickness, anger, and depression. At some point they will not be able to access the higher vibrational earth/Game. That's okay because it's not for you or me to judge, but rather to send them love. That might sound harsh but that might be their purpose in this Game—to be an example of a low vibe in order to assist others in evolving with the upgrade.

There is power in positivity and there is power in working together to raise the world's vibration. *Re.member* the Apollo 13 mission when the astronauts were in trouble? It seemed like there was no outcome possible where they would survive. The whole world was riveted, watching their story. People everywhere, from different countries and walks of life, prayed for them to make it back home. And it worked. Those men were able to pull off a miracle and make it back to Earth safe and sound. That's the power of unity.

The earth's vibration is increasing as you read this (look up the Schumann Resonances I mentioned earlier). Collectively we have the power to create heaven on earth together, so to speak, if we become unified with positive *intent.ions*, live a healthy lifestyle, and step into our true power. As one Game ends, a new one begins.

In the album *The Wild Places*, Dan Fogelberg talks about the "heaven on earth" that few people find. He points out that the "map's in your soul" and the road is already in your mind. You just need to follow it.

THE TRUTH YOU SHOULD KNOW

True power is hidden in plain sight, staring right at us. Why can't you see your true power? Because you are standing in the way. **You must be willing to go within to find what you want and who you want to be, not what society tells you to be.**

Society's traps of deception make us think material things like fame, power, control, and glory bring happiness. Those traps look delightful, like the poison apple in *Snow White*. Don't become one of those who stay in that trap for their whole life.

You can tap into your true power by being coherent and aligning your mind, body, and soul with your heart and your awareness. Let go of that ego mindset. Embrace the oneness of all living things and shine your inner light so bright, that it's felt by all.

Know your truth and speak it in a kind yet passionate way. Feel it in every cell inside you. Your true power should feel like a powerful force, a passion. It is the fire inside you waiting to create the reality you desire so that you can then do extraordinary things. It is the motivation that drives you to greatness and to teach others how to awaken the greatness within them. It's a high vibration frequency that is in the flow of rhythm with your intuition, guiding you along the way. When you are living within your true power, you can't help but want to start your day with *act.ion* steps because you live each day in a state of purpose, happiness and peace. Those *act.ion* steps might be sitting at the beach listening to waves, feeling the warm sun on your face, the sand between your toes, or it might be learning to take on society and expose the deception that has been fed to us, or a combination of both, depending on the day.

We all have the ability to step into our true power. Have faith and trust you are worthy of this amazing life and start stepping into yours today.

YOUR DASH ACT.ION

Stop wishing your life away and start casting your *intent.ions* into existence. When you say "I want a home on the beach," for example, the "want" tells your subconscious mind you want it someday but it's a *want*, not a fact, and therefore, it's something out of your reach.

When you say "I will have a home on the beach," this tells your subconscious this will happen at some point in the future but maybe not now. Your mind knows something else must happen before this other thing will happen. The mind is essentially waiting on something to happen.

When you say "I have," it sends the subconscious mind the message that this is a done deal. That allows the mind to align with the vibe that makes it happen. "I have a beach house in Destin, Florida," is a precise message to your mind, your vibe, and the Universe. Start operating with "I have."

THE POWER
OF WORDS

Did you ever hear the saying "sticks and stones may break my bones but words will never hurt me?" I heard this saying all the time when I was young. Guess what? It's a huge lie. Words can end relationships, start wars, bring lovers together, create life, end life, and more. Words are used to build a person up or force them to bow down.

Before you speak a word, you have a thought (this is why we want to "fine tune" our thoughts). You literally manifest your world with the words you use with yourself and others. Words are the Alpha and Omega. Besides carrying the sound of God, they carry the breath of God.

There is power in the words we speak because words are sound, which is vibration, which is also light, color, shapes, and sacred geometry. Scientists dissected matter to its core and discovered sound and vibration, which is what also makes up our words. This is profound. I hope you let this sink into your heart and give it some thought before the next time you say something.

Choose your words wisely.

CHAPTER 10

YOU ARE THE HERO
OF THE GAME

"Once we understand that *we are writing our own story*,
the game of life *changes completely*."

PURVI RANIGA

Before I learned everything I have shared in this book (and that I share in the study course I lead, available on my website, www. thegameoflife101.com), I was stuck in this period of my life where I was living on the sidelines. I was working very long hours, missing out on my kids' lives, eating too much junk food, constantly watching *tell.LIE.vision* programs to keep me distracted, and spending my time with friends gossiping and spreading a low vibe. I desperately wanted to feel alive again, but I was lost.

I didn't know how to get back in and start, not just playing the Game of Life, but actually *living* as my best possible self. I longed for a purpose. From time to time, I would pick up books that once motivated me, yet feel nothing when I flipped through them. I searched for videos that might spark a light inside me. But nothing happened and nothing changed. I just felt drained and exhausted, like I was caught in a constant loop of the same thing day in and day out.

We all need to pause from time to time in order to take a breath, regroup, and make a new plan, but we don't want to stay in that place for too long because it can easily become a trap. We get comfortable where we are at, operating with no real Game Plan. Years can pass by unnoticed while we are sitting on the sidelines instead of getting in the Game. That was what was happening to me. My pause was becoming a permanent stop.

One summer day, my friend Deb came over to visit. We started to reminisce about some of the good times we had had. She mentioned that she missed hearing me speak at events. She told me I had been an inspiration for others, and she encouraged me to do the same again.

I realized that I had felt alive back then. I'd had a passion for life. Deb and I would go to events and, literally, the most amazing things would happen. We knew we were in our power and the flow of life-force was strong in both of us. As we reminisced about the "good old days," I realized I missed that part of me, too.

That night I lay in bed thinking about the old me and *re.membered* the adage, *"Ask and you shall receive"*. So, I took ten long, deep breaths and said out loud: "I AM DONE BEING BORED, I DEMAND TO HAVE PASSION, ABUNDANCE, AND PURPOSE IN MY LIFE NOW!!! THANK YOU."

As I said this, I felt a vibration throughout my body. I repeated this exercise for several days. Each time I said it with more authority, more passion, more confidence in myself and my mission. I was open to any inspired *act.ions* that came along and a few days later, I received a nudge to listen to a book on audio. That book motivated me and made me even more open to whatever came my way.

A little while later, a video popped up about something I always wanted to learn and I dived in to learn as quickly as I could. I found that I was making friends with people who had similar interests and drive as I did. I was enthusiastic, excited, and so were those people around me. It was clear: the Law of Vibration attracts what we vibe out.

You have control over your life and you have the ability to make it amazing. Each of us are born to do something extraordinary. Whether that's being an amazing, loving mom, an artist who brightens the day of others, a coach, teacher, or a friend, whatever your purpose in this Game is, know that you are here right now for a purpose.

You are a hero in your own Game, don't play small, not even for a minute. You were meant to be extraordinary.

For too long, I was caught in a "Drifter" mindset, where I was just going through the motions of work and sleep. I was just kind of existing. When you do that, you start letting outside influences affect what your think, how you feel, and which *act. ions* you take.

Drifters can also be the kind of people who watch *tell.LIE.vision* endlessly, *be.LIE.ving* whatever news is being sold that week. No matter which news or channel they follow, there's always a portrayal of one side or the other as bad and that information infiltrates your brain. We all know that person who talks about an event on the news as if it was personal to them, as if they are the authority on the matter because they watched reports about it for hours on end and feel they are in the know. They are passionate about the outcome, even though the outcome literally has nothing to do with their life at all. That, my friend, is a distraction that creates a Drifter mentality, and it's very damaging on many levels.

Let's look at how to recognize Drifter mode so you can shift out of it **fast**:

1. Your alarm goes off, you hit snooze. Alarm goes off again, you hit snooze again, and keep repeating that until you need to rush out the door.

2. You don't have a Game Plan for the things you want to accomplish for the day, month, year(s).

3. The music playing in your head is irritating and chaotic, attracting the same back to you.

4. You keep putting off Dash Act.ions until some vague future date and do zero visualizations.

5. You don't spend time each day creating or doing breathing techniques, meditation/prayers, or physical exercise.

6. Too often you make poor decisions in eating and other life events.

7. You play the victim in the Game of Life and make a lot of excuses.

We've all been in Drifter mode at one time or another. Many things in the world are designed to keep us in that comfort zone on the couch. Learn to recognize these Drifter traps so you can make a quick shift. This book, with its Game Plan and Dash Act.ions, gives you the tools to play the Game with *intent.ion*.

I hope you know that you are worth it. The light within you is the true power that is hidden within your heart, just waiting for you to acknowledge its existence. Once you are aware of the light inside you, you can never un-know that wisdom and knowledge. Even if you choose not to turn it on at first, you just know it's there, kind of like a light switch. Take *intent.ional act.ions* and you flip that switch to *On*. That's when you begin mindfully playing the Game. Your desire to find truth increases and with each realization, your light grows stronger within. You are continually striving to reach a higher sphere of consciousness for the good of you and all mankind.

Whenever you doubt your value or feel Drifter mode creeping in, say these words aloud:

- I am important. I am a hero. I am powerful, kind, and generous.

- There is a definite purpose for my being here on this earth.

- Now is the time for me to step into my true power and be all I can be. I am grateful for the enlightenment that has been given to me, and I accept the greatness inside of me. And so it is, thank you.

Now, let's look at the difference with someone who is living their life with intention. When you have a Game Plan, you choose to play the Game of Life and succeed at it, which makes your daily *act.ions* change to *intent.ional act.ions*. When that happens, you raise your vibration and begin stepping into your true power. Each day you become more aligned with your purpose and desires.

One important thing to note: **The more you do this, the faster you will manifest your *intent.ions*.** Starting your own business, finding the right partner, moving into a fabulous home, changing the world for the better. Your Game Plan is the key to making those manifestations a reality. Simply changing how you start and end each day will help you shift your perceptions and ability to respond rather than *re.act*. The *intent.ional act.ions* you take to align with your purpose, desires, and best self will unfold naturally for you.

> Practice your Dash Act.ions daily—this is a powerful mindset that you are building. Make this enjoyable, something you look forward to each day.

When you are a Strategic Player, you have a Game Plan and your day goes like this:

1. Your alarm goes off, playing your motivational song. It's the first thing you hear to begin your day. (I like Fleetwood Mac's *Don't Stop* because he sings: about opening your *eYe*s and looking at the day; to see things in a different way.)

    a. It is beneficial to wake up at the same time each day, even on weekends.

2. You sit up in bed and do mindful breathing (whatever rocks your boat).

    a. For example: breathe in slow (with your tongue on the roof of mouth) and as you breathe out, allow your breath to make a sound (this is "Toning"). Cats purr, people Tone. Repeat throughout the day.

3. Say your prayers and/or do a meditation, then read your *written statement of the future you.*

   a. Be relaxed because that's the key for the successful use of visualization techniques. This is where you visualize your journey and see your movie unfolding, as if you are watching it now.

      i. Imagine you already are this version of you, with the business/home/friends/purpose or whatever else is in your strategy.

      ii. Ask for signs to confirm you are on the right path and give you direction.

      iii. Ask and imagine what you will do today to make a step toward this version of you.

      iv. Now, visualize the world of your desires, have a positive mindset, filled with compassion and love. All systems (spiritual, government, school, financial, healthy food and water, etc.) transformed for the benefit of mankind.

4. You give thanks for everything you have: health, family, love, home, pets, yard, etc. You are grateful and thankful throughout the day for opportunities, moments, people.

   a. I am grateful for and love my _____ _____.

5. Put on your protection for the day. As you get out of bed to start the day, imagine putting on your protection from all the negativity in the world. Your Armor of God, in other words, which is composed of:

   a. **Shoes of Readiness**– so each step you take prepares you for whatever comes, and you walk in faith and trust.

   b. **Belt of Truth** – so you can set *intent.ions* to see truth clearly all day and have the willingness to discover all that is hidden.

   c. **Breastplate of Righteousness** – so that all the *act.ions* you take today are done with virtue.

   d. **Shield of Faith** – so you can be surrounded and grounded in truth as you go through your day, and low vibes will fall to your feet and not penetrate your shield.

   e. **Helmet of Salvation** – so you go forth with assurance of knowing where you stand between good and evil; this protects you from powerful blows of doubt from evil.

   f. **sWORD of Spirit** – so the WORDS you speak to yourself and others is additional protection; be mindful, speak with a loving, compassionate and kind heart.

6. Choose your Dash Act.ion activity for the day, whether this is exercise, yoga, reading, journaling, meditating… whatever motivates you.

7. As you wash your face, brush your teeth, or shower, you imagine washing off the negative low vibes and stepping into the now you, with purpose, passion, and love in your heart. You *intent.ionally* set your vibe for the day by loudly speaking your desires for that day, week, month. This can be a short phrase, a few words, or a long mission statement of your purpose.

   When you do this, look at yourself in the mirror.

   a. Speak aloud so you can hear yourself because this sets the vibe inside you.

   b. Feel the words as you say them. Speak with authority and confidence.

   c. End with, "And so it is, thank you!"

8. At night, before you go to bed, you repeat the above steps and ask to *re.member* your dreams or have your future-self give you a sign to *re.member* upon waking up.

Look for Signs

There are signs everywhere, if you just open your mind to seeing them. Having an open, willing, and *intent.ional* mindset is vitally important for all aspects of life, but especially when you want signs to help point you in the right direction or to show you that you are on the right path.

For instance, I wanted to feel more gratitude in my life, so I asked the Universe to show me ways and opportunities to feel and experience gratitude. Whenever I ask for a sign, I always ask to be shown three times to confirm that it's a true sign. That day, I was waiting for a friend and I walked into a store to pass the time. I saw a shirt that had the word *Gratitude* on it, and ironically, there was only one left. I took it as a sign and bought the shirt. That day, my friend and I exchanged late Christmas gifts and she gave me a shirt with *Gratitude* written on it. Later that night, I was on social media and a message for a 90-day gratitude experiment popped into my feed. I reached out and joined the experiment (which ended up becoming a Game Changer).

Those signs helped me to see opportunities to feel gratitude, experience gratitude, and grow in my gratitude for my life and the people around me. There are literally dozens of times when I have asked for a sign and there was one right in front of me.

There is no such thing as coincidence. These moments are signs from the Universe. Pay attention to them.

I have learned a lot over the years as I have begun to build and implement my own Game Plan for the Game of Life. There are no hard and fast rules; simply be in the flow and concentrate on having positive vibes and you will be on the right path. Always trust your heart and your intuition, not someone else's.

The amount of time you spend on any of these *act.ions* is up to you. As you get into the rhythm of doing these *act.ions*, you may want to get up earlier and spend more time on things like meditation or manifestation because it feels good, and you are seeing results. *Re.member*, the more you do this, the quicker you will manifest your *intent.ions*.

Re.member, you are the hero of this Game of Life; it's your movie and your song. OWN IT.

If you are struggling to stay on track, create an environment that reminds you of your *intent.ions*. Write down your visualizations, your Dash Act.ions, maybe a reminder to just breathe, or a few motivational words and phrases on note cards. Then put these reminders by your bed, on mirrors, on your desk, etc.

When you ask the Universe for anything, live as if it is already done. Give thanks for this blessing and be excited. Always be open and flexible. **If you are not flexible, you are breakable.**

I want to thank you and congratulate you for picking up this book and embarking on a new way of playing the Game of Life. You have taken a huge step forward in realizing your true power and becoming the hero that is alive inside you.

The Game is not over yet, though! Head on over to my website (www.thegameoflife101.com) and discover a few Game Tokens that I have created for you to help you keep the momentum of this journey going. You will also find a summary of all the Dash Act.ions to help guide you through the Game. Download it to keep as a reference to reflect back on daily or as needed. You'll find guidance and resources to create your own Game Plan and to start leveling up right this second.

Check out www.thegameoflife101.com for all that and other great resources, like the Game Plan with Dash Act.ion workbook, empowerment calls, HeartMath Resilience Advantage sessions, law common to i, coaching, TAM-IT study courses, plus much, much more.

THE GAME OF LIFE CHEAT SHEET

This is designed to be a short and sweet "cheat sheet" reminding you of how things flow and how to become your best self. When you are pressed for time or need a quick refresher, let this be your go-to for embracing the true power of your life-force and succeeding in this Game of Life. By using these tips and the Dash Act.ions daily, you will manifest that which you set your *intent.ions* on and have the life you always imagined and envisioned of having. *Re.member* the analogy of the guitar string that I showed you on page 79 as you work through these tips.

CHANGE YOUR *E.MOTIONS*

- Your *e.motions* trigger the vibe you emit to the Universe, affecting everyone around you in a powerful way.

- Don't get emotionally attached to *be.LIE.fs* you have learned. Just because you were taught them doesn't mean they are true. Maintain the ability to challenge everything you know; be open and willing to question your core *be.LIE.fs*, even if you discover what you thought was a truth is actually a lie. You will be fine. Life still goes on.

- Research and study the Natural Laws. Once you inner-stand them, you will see the miracles that surround you.

- Shift your consciousness and begin to see things differently. Inner-stand another person's viewpoint. Let go of your negative vibes, negative people, and past traumas.

- Choose to see the good in all moments. There is always something good.

- *Re.member*, **you control you**. Respond rather than *re.act*.

CONTROL YOUR THOUGHTS

- Break the chains on your mind. Think about things in a new way.

- Realize and know that we are all equal in the Game of Life (titles are fictitious); don't give away your power to another.

- Start your day by setting your *intent.ions* to create a shift inside you to get your desired results.

- Mindfully choose the vibration you want to send out to the Universe.

- Let your imagination and intuition direct your moves in the Game.

- Set a time limit on feeling stuck or sad, then choose to change your thoughts for a positive and loving path forward.

TAKE *INTENT.IONAL ACT.IONS*

- Start your day with a Game Plan of *act.ions* that bring you closer to align with your purpose.

- Don't be the Drifter; create an *intent.ional act.ion* whenever you feel stuck in a trap or find yourself just going through the motions.

- Live your legacy now. Be the person you want others to *re.member*. Be the person who makes a difference. How would that person act or speak?

- Create your life tribute.

- Say I love you often, forgive endlessly, repent for your errors, and be of service to others.

Don't just close this book and go back to ordinary life. You picked up this book for a reason. Let that reason be the force that guides your *e.motions*, thoughts, and *act.ions* today and every day going forward.

As we come to the end of this book and reflect back on this journey in the Game, I want to share a quote that summarizes the *intent.ions* of this book perfectly:

"Life is a matter of choice. Everything we manifest in our day-to-day lives is the direct result of our choices along the way. Each choice automatically creates a consequence. From our choices other people's lives are influenced for better or worse."

DANNION BRINKLEY

Thank you for your time and sharing this part of your Game of Life with me. You are special and have a definite purpose. Step into your true power and enjoy the Game!

ABOUT
THE AUTHOR

Ever since she was young, Kathleen Acker Ramsey envisioned herself empowering others and helping them along the playful, healing, spiritual and yet logical journey of playing the Game of Life. Kathleen's own life has been a rollercoaster of escape from abuse, multiple moves, and life changes but throughout it all she has continued to seek the best way to live her life in order to find meaning and satisfaction.

Kathleen has a strong logical side, with more than thirty years of experience in the legal field, and has successfully completed negotiations for many top global companies. She is continually striving to learn more by her life-long journey of taking classes, attending retreats, acquiring licenses and certifications, plus empowering her own spiritual growth. She has devoted her life to sharing the transformational power that an innovative, impactful mindset can bring to life.

She lives in the St. Louis area with her two sons, two dogs and cat. She's an avid reader, spiritual seeker of truth, faith in God, and most of all a strong woman who strives to be the change she desires to see in our world.

www.ingramcontent.com/pod-product-compliance
Lightning Source LLC
Chambersburg PA
CBHW051513120626
46551CB00012B/906